What Is Globalization?

Ulrich Beck

Translated by Patrick Camiller

polity

Copyright © this translation Polity Press.

First published in Germany as *Was ist Globalisierung?* © Suhrkamp Verlag, 1997.

First published in 2000 by Polity Press in association with
Blackwell Publishers, a Blackwell Publishing Company

Reprinted 2000 (twice), 2001, 2002, 2003, 2004, 2005

Published with the assistance of Inter Nationes.

Polity Press
65 Bridge Street
Cambridge CB2 1UR, UK

Polity Press
350 Main Street
Malden, MA 02148, USA

A catalogue record for this book is available from the British Library.

Library of Congress Cataloging-in-Publication Data

Beck, Ulrich, 1944–
    [Was ist Globalisierung? English]
    What Is globalization? / Ulrich Beck; translated by Patrick Camiller.
        p.   cm.
    Includes bibliographical references and index.
    ISBN 0–7456–2125–2 (hb.).—ISBN 0–7456–2126–0 (pb.)
    1. International economic relations.   2. International relations.
    I. Title.
HF 1359.B413   2000
337—dc21   99-27522
                                                                        CIP

Typeset in 10.5 on 12pt Palatino
by Kolam Information Services Pvt. Ltd, Pondicherry, India
Printed in Great Britain by MPG Books Ltd, Bodmin, Cornwall

This book is printed on acid-free paper.

For further information on Polity, please visit our website:
http://www.polity.co.uk

Contents

Preface

The purpose of this book is to offer a trenchant introduction that will assist readers facing the thorny paths of the globalization debate: to clarify its ambiguities of fact and value, and to distinguish more clearly than is usually the case between its various dimensions. Another aim is to warn of a number of conceptual pitfalls, but the most important of all is to open up the horizon for political responses to globalization. Two questions, then, each difficult in its simplicity, will be at the centre of attention. What does globalization mean? How can it be moulded politically?

In connection with this essay, two Readers have been produced in German in which the various arguments, conclusions and controversies regarding globalization are documented and presented with the help of 'classical' and more recent texts. The titles of these volumes are: *Politik der Globalisierung* [Politics of Globalization] and *Perspektiven der Weltgesellschaft – Kontroversen, Konflikte, Paradoxien* [Perspectives for World Society: Controversies, Conflicts, Paradoxes].

I began work on these volumes two years ago, and their completion was made possible above all by a Distinguished Research professorship that I took up at the University of Wales, Cardiff, in the winter semester of 1995–6. Without the extremely stimulating discussions I had with Barbara Adam, Martin Albrow, Jörg Dürrschmidt, Anthony Giddens, David Held, Scott Lash, John Thompson, Robin White-Grove, Helen Wilkinson, Brian Wynne and many others – but most of all, as ever, with Elisabeth Beck-Gernsheim – this book would never have seen the light of day. I would like to express here my deepest gratitude to them all.

Acknowledgements

The author and publisher gratefully acknowledge permission to reprint from the following:

Zygmunt Bauman: from *Globalization* (Polity Press, 1998), by permission of the publisher.

Charlotte Bretherton: from 'Universal Human Rights: Bringing People into Global Politics', in C. Bretherton and G. Ponton (eds), *Global Politics* (Blackwell, 1996), by permission of the publisher.

J. N. Pieterse: from 'Globalization as Hybridization', in M. Featherstone, S. Lash and R. Robertson (eds), *Global Modernities* (Sage, 1995), by permission of Sage Publications Ltd and the author.

Martin Shaw: from *Civil Society and the Media in Global Crises: representing distant violence* (Pinter, 1996), by permission of Cassell & Co.

Andreas Zielcke: extract from 'Der Neue Doppelgänger', in the *Frankfurter Allgemeine Zeitung*, 20 July 1996, by permission of the Frankfurter Allgemeine Zeitung.

Introduction

Virtual taxpayers

With the peaceful fall of the Berlin Wall and the collapse of the Soviet empire, many thought that the end of politics was nigh as we entered an age beyond socialism and capitalism, utopia and emancipation. In the years since then, however, the ceremonial farewells to politics have become rather more subdued. The current scare-word 'globalization', seemingly unavoidable in any public statement, points not to an end of politics but to its *escape* from the categories of the national state, and even from the schema defining what is 'political' and 'non-political' action. For whatever the referent of the new globalization rhetoric (economy, markets, job competition, production, goods and services, financial flows, information, lifestyles), the political consequences of the stage-managed *economic* globalization risk stand out in sharp relief. Institutions of industrial society which seemed shut tight can be 'cracked' and opened up to political intervention. The premises of the welfare state and pension system, of income support, local government and infrastructural policies, the power of organized labour, industry-wide free collective bargaining, state expenditure, the fiscal system and 'fair taxation' – all this melts under the withering sun of globalization and becomes susceptible to (demands for) political moulding. Every social actor must respond in one way or another; and the typical responses do *not* fit into the old left–right schema of political action.[1]

We may say that what used to be the class question for the workers' movement in the nineteenth century is the globalization question for transnationally active enterprises at the turn of the twenty-first century – but with the crucial difference that the workers' movement acted as a *countervailing* power, whereas global enterprises have for a long time *not* been challenged by any other (transnational) power.

Why then does globalization mean politicization? It means this because the staging of globalization permits employers and their associations to disentangle and recapture their power to act that was restrained by the political and welfare institutions of democratically organized capitalism. Globalization makes possible things which, though perhaps always there, remained hidden during the stage of the welfare-democratic taming of capitalism. It means that corporations, especially globally active ones, can play a key role in shaping not only the economy but society as whole – if 'only' because they have it in their power to withdraw the material resources (capital, taxes, jobs) from society.

The global operation of the economy is sapping the foundations of national economics and national states, unleashing subpolitics on a quite novel scale and with incalculable consequences. The next objective will be to shunt the old adversary, 'labour', out of harm's way, but above all to serve notice on the 'ideal aggregate capitalist' (as Marx called the *state*) so that it is freed from the entanglement with labour and state that developed in the course of the nineteenth and twentieth centuries.

'All fixed, fast-frozen relations, with their train of ancient and venerable prejudices and opinions, are swept away' – Marx, already in the *Communist Manifesto*, hardly kept secret his celebration of the revolutionary potential of capital. Today the 'fixed and fast-frozen' is the welfare-state and trade-union organization of labour, while the 'ancient and venerable' are the bureaucratic prescriptions and fiscal exactions of the (national) state. Efficiency and neatness, then, will result from a novel politics based upon the 'material constraints' of globalization.

All around, one hears the assertion that it is not corporate interests but 'globalization' which forces this or that painful break with the past. One of the 'laws' of the global market is that not-A must be done in order to achieve A: for example, that jobs must be axed or relocated in order to keep jobs safe where they are. Precisely because labour can and must be downsized to boost profits, current policies are twisted until they appear as their opposite. Thus, to stimulate economic growth is ultimately to 'produce' unemployment; and to cut taxes so that profit opportunities improve might possibly also 'produce' unemployment. The political and social paradoxes of a transnational economy – which must be lured and rewarded with the 'removal of barriers to investment' (meaning the removal of ecological, union, welfare and fiscal constraints), so that more and more labour can be *shed* and output and profits simultaneously increased – still have to be scientifically analysed and politically tackled.

Globalization policies featuring an orchestrated global scare are thus intended to shake off the fetters not only of trade unions but also of the national state, to deprive national politics as such of its power. The rhetoric hurled at welfare-state policies by major figures in the economy makes it as clear as one could wish that the final aim is to dismantle the existing responsibilities and apparatus of the state, to bring about the anarchistic market utopia of a *minimal* state. Paradoxically, however, it is also the case that globalization is often answered with *re*-nationalization.

Politicians from various parties do not realize that the very substance of politics and the state, as well as of the trade unions, is at stake in the globalization campaign. Surprised and fascinated by the power of globalization to 'soften up' institutions, they are only just beginning to suspect that – as Marx put it long ago – they are supposed to become their own gravediggers. It cannot but seem ironical, to this author at least, that some politicians call for ever freer markets without even noticing that this threatens their own lifeblood, the very source of their money and power. Has such gay abandon ever been seen before at an act of public suicide?

What is the basis of the new power of the transnationals? How is it that their strategic potential is growing larger?

Without a revolution, without even any change in laws or constitutions, an attack has been launched 'in the normal course of business', as it were, upon the material lifelines of modern national societies.

First, the transnational corporations are able to *export jobs* to parts of the world where labour costs and workplace obligations are lowest.

Second, the computer-generation of worldwide proximity enables them to break down and disperse goods and services, and to produce them *through a division of labour in different parts of the world*, so that national and corporate labels inevitably become illusory.

Third, they are in a position to play off countries or individual locations against one another, in a process of 'global horse-trading' to find the cheapest fiscal conditions and the most favourable infrastructure. They can also 'punish' particular countries if they seem too 'expensive' or 'investment-unfriendly'.

Fourth and last, in the manufactured and controlled jungle of global production, they are able *to decide for themselves their investment site, production site, tax site and residence site*, and to play these off against one another. As a result, top executives can live where it is nicest to live, and pay taxes where it is cheapest.

All this has come to pass without any complaint or discussion in parliaments, without any decision by governments and without any change in the law; nor has any public debate been necessary. This justifies us in speaking of a 'subpolitics'[2] – not to suggest some conspiracy theory, but to indicate that corporations acting within the framework of world society have gained additional scope for action and power *beyond* the political system. Over the heads of government and parliament, public opinion and the courts, the balance-of-power contract that characterized the first modernity of industrial society is now being terminated and transferred to the *independent realm* of economic action. The transition to a politics of globalization has crept in on velvet paws, under the guise of normality, rewriting the societal rules of the game – with the legitimacy of a modernization that will happen come what may.

The national state is a territorial state: that is, its power is grounded upon attachment to a particular place (upon control over membership, current legislation, border defence, and so on). The world society which, in the wake of globalization, has taken shape in many (not only economic) dimensions is undermining the importance of the national state, because a multiplicity of social circles, communication networks, market relations and lifestyles, none of them specific to any particular locality, now cut across the boundaries of the national state. This is apparent in each of the pillars of sovereignty: in tax-raising, police responsibilities, foreign policy and military security. Let us take the example of taxes.

The levying of taxes concerns not just one principle but *the* principle underlying the authority of the national state. This right to levy taxes is linked to the supervision of economic activities within a certain territory, but it is becoming an ever more fictitious basis as the scope increases for operations at the level of world society. Companies can produce in one country, pay taxes in another and demand state infrastructural spending in yet another. People too have become more mobile. If they are rich, they prove more adept at exploiting holes in the fiscal nets of the state; if they have sought-after job skills, they deploy them where they stand to gain most; and if they are poor, they set off for places where milk and honey beckon. On the other hand, national states become increasingly entangled in contradictions if they try to shut themselves off from the rest of the world. For they must all attract capital, people and knowledge in order to survive the competition in world society.

The gladiators of economic growth who are so courted by politicians erode the authority of the state by demanding its services whilst denying it tax revenue. The point is that it is precisely the super-rich who become *virtual taxpayers*, and their riches rest not least upon this virtue of the virtual. In ways that are (mostly) legal yet illegitimate, they undermine the democratic public good of which they take advantage.

Fortune magazine, which regularly publishes a league table of the world's top 500 companies, jubilantly reports that these have been 'pushing across frontiers to capture new markets and swallow up the local competition. Their guiding idea is: the more countries, the greater the profits. And indeed the profits of the top 500 have risen by 15 per cent, with an increase in turnover of only 11 per cent.'[3]

'Profits up, jobs out,' runs an article title in *Der Spiegel*: 'A special kind of economic miracle is striking fear into the nation. A new generation of corporate bosses have taken over and are embracing American-style share worship. Worst of all, the stock market is rewarding job killers.'[4]

Businessmen have discovered the road to riches. The new magic formula is: capitalism *without work* plus capitalism *without taxes*. Between 1989 and 1993, the tax yield from corporate profits fell by 18.6 per cent, and by nearly a half as a proportion of total fiscal revenue.

André Gorz argues:

The social security system must be reorganized, and new foundations put in its place. But we must also ask why it seems to have become impossible to finance this reconstruction. Over the past twenty years, the EU countries have become 50 to 70 per cent richer. The economy has grown much faster than the population. Yet the EU now has twenty million unemployed, fifty million below the poverty line and five million homeless. What has happened to the extra wealth? From the case of the United States, we know that economic growth has enriched only the best-off 10 per cent of the population. This 10 per cent has garnered 96 per cent of the additional wealth. Things are not quite as bad in Europe, but they are not much better.

In Germany since 1979 corporate profits have risen by 90 per cent and wages by 6 per cent. But revenue from income tax has doubled over the past ten years, while revenue from corporate taxes has fallen by a half. It now contributes a mere 13 per cent of total tax revenue, down from 25 per cent in 1980 and 35 per cent in 1960. Had the figure remained at 25 per cent, the state would have annually netted an extra 86 billion marks in recent years.

Developments have been similar in other countries. Most transnational corporations like Siemens or BMW no longer pay any taxes at home. [...] Unless there is some change here [...] people will rightly not accept cuts in their social services, pensions and take-home pay.[5]

Transnational corporations (TNCs) are securing record profits – and a massive downsizing of labour. Chairmen's annual reports present one dream balance after another. But politicians who have to justify scandalous levels of unemployment push for further tax cuts, in the mostly vain hope that at least a few jobs will be squeezed from the new wealth of the rich.

The social barometer is therefore showing a rise in conflicts, including between virtual and real taxpayers. Whereas TNCs can escape the clutches of inland revenue bureaucracies, small and medium-sized companies (which create a large share of new jobs) have to cough up more and more as the screws are turned on them. It is an irony of history that the very *losers* of globalization will in future have to pay for everything – from the welfare state to a functioning democracy – while the *winners* of globalization post dream profits and steal away from their responsibility for future democracy. It follows that, in the age of globalization, the major issue of social justice will have to be handled in a new way, both theoretically and politically.

But the contradictions of 'jobless capitalism' are also becoming easier to perceive. Managers may transfer the administration of transnational companies to southern India, yet send their children to the top publicly funded European universities. It never crosses their mind to move to where they are building up jobs and paying low taxes. For themselves they demand high-cost political, social and civil rights as a matter of course, while torpedoing the public finances that support them. They go to the theatre. They enjoy well-cared-for nature and landscape. They romp around the still relatively crime-free cities of Europe. But their profit-oriented policies are doing a lot to ensure that this European way of life will fall apart. Might we know where they or their children want to live when the state and democracy can no longer be paid for in Europe?

What is good for the Deutsche Bank has for a long time not been good for Germany. The TNCs are bidding farewell to the framework of the national state and refusing further loyalty to its actors. This, however, lowers the degree of *internal* social integration, all the more so as its basis was purely economic. It is precisely the well-endowed welfare states which are facing the worst predicament. They have to provide statutory benefits for an ever higher number of registered unemployed (fast approaching five million in Germany), and at the same time they lose control over taxes because the TNCs deal themselves a quite unparalleled hand in the poker game over their local ties and obligations. Or, to change the metaphor, they have four bites at the cherry: first, by gaining the best possible access to quality infrastructure; second, by picking up various subsidies; third, by reducing their tax burden to a minimum; and fourth, by externalizing the costs of the unemployed.

The downward pressure on the welfare state, then, results not only from a combination of dwindling resources and rocketing expenditure, but also from the fact that it lacks the means to satisfy demands upon it at a time when the gulf between rich and poor is growing ever wider. As the national framework loses its binding force, the winners and the losers of globalization cease to sit at the same table. The new rich no longer 'need' the new poor. And so it becomes increasingly difficult to even out the differences between them, because there is no framework in which this overarching conflict could be represented and regulated.[6]

It is not hard to see what this entails. The conflictual logic of the capitalist zero-sum game has been re-emerging and growing sharper, while the state has been losing its customary means to pacify and conciliate by increasing the size of the economic cake available for distribution.

A question mark thus appears over the model of the first, national modernity, which was conceived and organized within a particular cultural identity (a 'people'), a territory and a state. At the same time, however, no new unity of humanity, planet earth and world state has become visible or even desirable to large numbers of people.

The national state caught between world economy and individualization: what is to be done?

The conclusion seems to suggest itself that the project of modernity has failed. The philosophers of 'postmodernism' were the first to issue a spirited death certificate for the rationality claims of science, arguing that what passed itself off in the West as the universalism of Enlightenment and human rights was nothing other than the voice of 'dead old white males' who had trampled on the rights of ethnic, religious and sexual minorities by absolutizing their own partisan 'meta-narrative'.

It is further argued that the social cement has grown porous through the secular trend of *individualization*, that society has been losing its collective self-consciousness and therefore its capacity for political action. The quest for political responses to the great issues of the future no longer has any subject or any locus.

In this pitch-dark view of things, economic globalization merely completes what has been driven forward intellectually by postmodernism and politically by individualization: namely, the collapse of modernity. The diagnosis points towards a *capitalism without work* that will *create unemployment on a huge scale*; the historical association between market economy, welfare state and democracy, the Western model that integrated and legitimated the nation-state project of modernity, is thus destined to break down. According to this scenario, neoliberals are the liquidators of the West – even if they set themselves up as its reformers. As far as the welfare state, democracy and a public sphere are concerned, they are pursuing a course of modernization to the death.

But decline begins in the head. Fatalism is also a language disorder. And before jumping off the Eiffel Tower, one really ought to consult a language therapist. 'Concepts are empty: they no longer grip, illuminate or inflame. The greyness lying over the world [...] may also come from a kind of verbal mildew.'[7] What appears as collapse might, if it succeeds in overcoming the fatal orthodoxies of the first modernity, open out into a second modernity.[8]

In my book *Kinder der Freiheit*, I tried to show that with the so-called 'collapse of values' it was perhaps the collective orthodoxy of political action but not political action as such that was coming to an end. In other words, as social-moral milieux have faded away, foundations have developed in the lifeworld for a *cosmopolitan republicanism* centred on freedom of the individual.

Nevertheless, it is difficult to speak out against the world power of the world market. This is possible only by destroying the image of an all-powerful world market that rules in people's heads and cripples all action. In this book I would like to oppose that mega-spectre haunting Europe, and to do so with the slingshot of a distinction between *globalism* on the one hand, and *globality* and *globalization* on the other. This distinction is designed to break up the *territorial orthodoxy of the political and the social*, posed in absolute institutional categories, which arose with the national-state project of the first modernity.

By *globalism* I mean the view that the world market eliminates or supplants political action – that is, the ideology of rule by the world market, the ideology of neoliberalism. It proceeds monocausally and economistically, reducing the multidimensionality of globalization to a single, economic dimension that is itself conceived in a linear fashion. If it mentions at all the other dimensions of globalization – ecology, culture, politics, civil society – it does so only by placing them under the sway of the world-market system. Of course, there can be no denying the central importance of economic globalization, also as an option and perception of corporate players. But the ideological core of globalism is that a basic difference of the first modernity is hereby liquidated, that is, the difference between politics and economics. The central task of politics, which is to define the basic legal, social and ecological conditions under which economic activity first becomes socially possible and legitimate, drops out of view or is suppressed. Globalism implies that a complex structure such as Germany – its state, its society, its culture, its foreign policy – can be run in the way that a company is run. But this involves a veritable imperialism of economics, where companies demand the basic conditions under which they can optimize their goals.

The striking thing is that globalism, understood in this way, casts its spell even over its opponents. Along with affirmative globalism, there is also a 'negative' globalism which, having been convinced of the inescapable dominance of the world market, takes refuge in various forms of protectionism.

Conservative protectionists bewail the collapse of values and the declining significance of the national dimension, but rather contradictorily also pursue the neoliberal destruction of the national state.

Green protectionists see the national state as a political biotope threatened with extinction, which upholds environmental standards against world-market forces and is thus as deserving of protection as nature itself.

Red protectionists don for every case the dusted-down costume of class struggle; globalization is another word for 'right after all' as they celebrate their Marxist feast of the resurrection. However, it is a 'being right' that is afflicted with utopian blindness.

These pitfalls of globalism should be distinguished from what I would like to call – in tune with Anglo-American discussion – globality and globalization.

Globality means that *we have been living for a long time in a world society*, in the sense that the notion of closed spaces has become illusory. No country or group can shut itself off from others. Various economic, cultural and political forms therefore collide with one another, and things that used to be taken for granted (including in the Western model) will have to be justified anew. 'World society', then, denotes the totality of social relationships which are *not* integrated into or determined (or determinable) by national-state politics. Self-perceptions, as staged by the national mass media, here play a crucial role, so that world society in the narrower sense – to propose a still politically relevant operational criterion – means *perceived* or *reflexive* world society. The question of how far it exists may therefore (in accordance with the Thomas theorem that what people believe to be real becomes real in its consequences) be empirically turned into the question of how, and to what extent, people and cultures around the world relate to one another in their differences, and to what extent this self-perception of world society is relevant to how they behave.[9]

'World' in the combination 'world society' thus means *difference* or *multiplicity*, and 'society' means *non*-integration, so that we may (together with M. Albrow) conceive world society as *multiplicity without unity*. As we shall see, this presupposes a number of very different things: transnational forms of production and labour market competition, global reporting in the media, transnational consumer boycotts, transnational ways of life, as well as 'globally' perceived crises and wars, military and peaceful use of atomic energy, destruction of nature, and so on.

Globalization, on the other hand, denotes the *processes* through which sovereign national states are criss-crossed and undermined by transnational actors with varying prospects of power, orientations, identities and networks.

One essential feature distinguishing the second from the first modernity is the fact that *the new globality cannot be reversed*. This means that the various autonomous logics of globalization – the logics of ecology, culture, economics, politics and civil society – exist side by side and cannot be reduced or collapsed into one another. Rather, each must be independently decoded and grasped in its interdependences. The guiding supposition is that only in this way can the perspective and the space for political action be opened up. Why? Because only then can the depoliticizing spell of globalism be broken; only with a multidimensional view of globality can the globalist ideology of 'material compulsion' be broken down. But what is it that makes globality irreversible? Eight reasons may be given under the following headings:

1 The geographical expansion and ever greater density of international trade, as well as the global networking of finance markets and the growing power of transnational corporations.
2 The ongoing revolution of information and communications technology.
3 The universal *demands* for human rights – the (lip service paid to the) principle of democracy.
4 The stream of images from the global culture industries.
5 The emergence of a postnational, polycentric world politics, in which transnational actors (corporations, non-governmental organizations, United Nations) are growing in power and number alongside governments.
6 The question of world poverty.
7 The issue of global environmental destruction.
8 Transcultural conflicts in one and the same place.

In these circumstances, sociology acquires new significance as an exploration of what human life means in the trap that the world has become. Globality means that from now on nothing which happens on our planet is only a limited local event; all inventions, victories and catastrophes affect the whole world, and we must reorient and reorganize our lives and actions, our organizations and institutions, along a 'local–global' axis. Globality, understood in this way, denotes the new situation of the second modernity. This concept also concentrates elementary reasons why the stock answers of the first modernity are inapplicable and contradictory for the second modernity, where politics will have to be refounded or reinvented.

This concept of globality may be distinguished from the concept of a *globalization process* (a dialectical process, one would say in old-fashioned language), which creates transnational social links and spaces, revalues local cultures and promotes third cultures ('a little of this, a little of that, is the way new things come into the world' – Salman Rushdie). Within this complex framework, the question of the *extent* of successful globalization as well as of its *limits* may be posed anew in relation to three parameters: (a) extension in *space*; (b) stability over *time*; and (c) social *density* of the transnational networks, relationships and image-flows.

This conceptual horizon makes it possible to answer a further question: namely, what is historically specific about contemporary globalization and its paradoxes at a particular place (for example, in comparison with the 'capitalist world-system' that was already under construction in the age of colonialism)?[10]

The peculiarity of the present, and future, globalization process lies in the empirically ascertainable *scale, density and stability of regional–global relationship networks and their self-definition through the mass media, as well as of social spaces and of image-flows at a cultural, political, economic and military level.*[11] World society is thus not a mega-national society containing and dissolving all national societies within itself, but a world horizon characterized by multiplicity and non-integration which opens out when it is produced and preserved in communication and action.

Sceptics will ask what is new about this, and answer: nothing really important. But they are wrong: historically, empirically and theoretically. What is new is not only the everyday life and inter-action across national frontiers, in dense networks with a high degree of mutual dependence and obligation. New, too, is the self-perception of this transnationality (in the mass media, con-sumption or tourism); new is the 'placelessness' of community, labour and capital; new are the awareness of global ecological dangers and the corresponding arenas of action; new is the ines-capable perception of transcultural Others in one's own life, with all the contradictory certainties resulting from it; new is the level at which 'global culture industries' circulate (Scott Lash and John Urry); new are the rise of a European structure of states, and the number and power of transnational actors, institutions and agreements; and new, finally, is the degree of economic concentration, which is nevertheless slowed down by cross-frontier competition in the world market.

Globalization, then, also means *no* world state – or, to be more precise, world society *without a world state* and *without world government*. A globally *disorganized* capitalism is continually spreading out. For there is no hegemonic power and no international regime, either economic or political.

The distinction made in this Introduction provides the framework for this book. In Part I – 'Dimensions, Controversies, Definitions' – multidimensionality and the ambivalences and paradoxes of globality and globalization are sketched out and contrasted with one another, in respect of society, economics, politics, ecology and culture.

In Part II – 'Perspectives' – it will be shown in chapter 4 that creative space for the primacy of politics can be regained only through a decisive critique of globalism. In chapters 5 and 6 – 'Responses to Globalization' and 'Europe and Globalization' – a kind of public brainstorming will try to counter the prevailing paralysis of politics and offer ten ways of beginning to address and answer the challenges of the global age.

The Conclusion, a kind of Cassandrist finger exercise, then considers what will happen if nothing happens: the 'Brazilianization of Europe'.

The globalization shock: a belated discussion

The debate on globalization which is now shaking public life has arrived in Germany with some delay. In Britain, for example, a lively and productive discussion of the 'G word' has been taking place for more than ten years, right across the political parties and with the participation of economists, historians, and social and political scientists. All the greater is the *globalization shock* in Germany.

One of the reasons for this is that, according to the dominant view in Germany, globalization is mainly associated with a cutback in indigenous jobs and their relocation in low-wage countries – at a time when German society, despite economic growth and soaring profits for TNCs, has to endure mass unemployment more reminiscent of the Weimar period.

Four further reasons may be identified, however, for the political shock that globalization has dealt to Central Europe, France, Austria, Switzerland, Italy and, above all, Germany.

First, states and societies with a primarily economic consciousness of themselves – 'deutschmark nationalism', 'export nation', etc. – feel especially endangered by a world-market globalization supposedly coming from outside.

Second, for countries such as France or Germany, where, unlike in the USA or Britain, the state is caught up in extensive social commitments, the age of globalization represents a double bind. As economic development escapes the control of national states, the social consequences – unemployment, migration, poverty – cluster together in their welfare safety-nets.

Third, globalization shakes to its foundations the self-image of a homogeneous, self-contained national space calling itself the Federal Republic. By contrast, Great Britain used to be the centre of a world empire, and globalization brings back some fond memories. It is true that for many years Germany has also been a global location where the world's cultures and contradictions disport themselves. But till now this reality has been obscured in the self-image of a largely homogeneous nation. All this then came to light as a result of the globalization debate. For, as we have seen, globalization means one thing above all else: *de*nationalization – that is, erosion of the national state, but also its possible transformation into a transnational state.

Fourth, not only does this 'denationalization shock' call into question the key categories of postwar German identity, the corporatist 'German model' and its special social system; the whole experience and challenge also conflict with the disputes surrounding the unification of the two Germanies. For the unification drama (in many ways comparable to a marital drama) forced the Germans into a preoccupation with themselves. After a half-century of living apart, the question posed itself of what remained common to 'Germans' as such, and whether it was really worth identifying with the others. It was during this phase of self-contemplation and self-questioning that the news of globalization burst on the country. Over and above the planned transfer of powers within the European Union, it seemed that the national state was to lose its sovereignty and substance in every dimension: financial resources, the power to shape things politically and economically, information and cultural policy, ordinary civic identity. The question of how 'transnational states' *might* arise in response to globalization,[12] of what this might mean economically, militarily, politically and culturally, was discussed to only a small extent.

In the dizzying *annus mirabilis* of 1989 people still said: 'What belongs together is growing together' (Willy Brandt). But now the message of the globalization debate is that those hopes – and their disappointments – rested upon an obsolete image of the national idyll. If the traditional model of the national state is to have any chance of survival at all in the new power structure of world market plus transnational actors and movements, the globalization process will have to become the criterion of national politics in every domain (in economics, law, military affairs, and so on).

It is not up to the individual, or to social and political actors, whether they recognize this or not. The new developments in world society, which are making the idea of 'national' products, firms, technologies, industries or even sports associations increasingly fictitious, *compel* them on pain of economic, political and cultural decline to open their eyes to the possibilities, ideologies, paradoxes and hysterias of the global age – and above all, to the new power game to which everyone is to a greater or lesser degree subjected. To put it in another way, *globality is an unavoidable condition of human intercourse at the close of the twentieth century*.

The bases of the first modernity must therefore be renegotiated. What does tolerance mean? What do supposedly universal human rights involve in a context of cultural difference? Who will uphold human rights in a world that has left behind the national state? How can social safeguards that have been overwhelmingly guaranteed by the national state be redrawn and preserved amid increasing world poverty and a decline in paid employment? If national states crumble, will new wars of religion ensue, perhaps intensified by ecological disasters? Or are we heading towards a world without violence, finally at peace after the triumph of the world market? Are we perhaps even on the threshold of a second Enlightenment?

All this comes up in the wake of the globalization debate. But no one knows, or can know, how such questions affecting the core of civilization can be answered across the trenches that divide rich and poor, ethnic groups, continents or religions, each with their complex histories of violence.

PART I
Dimensions, Controversies, Definitions

The counter-revolution fails   At the time when the Soviet empire was falling apart, Boris Yeltsin – who was then President of the Russian Federation – addressed the people of Moscow in a spirited speech against the Communist putschists from the top of an armoured car, a speech broadcast not by Soviet Radio (which was in the hands of the old Communists) but via CNN satellite. At that decisive moment in history, the spectacular significance of a global information network, symbolized by satellites, became readily discernible as national sovereignty over information ceased to apply as a part of political sovereignty. National states can no longer cut themselves off from one another; their army-patrolled frontiers are full of holes, at least as far as their insertion in the space of global communications is concerned: *informational globalization*

Toxic penguin meat   Much earlier, in the 1960s, biologists found in penguin meat in Antarctica high concentrations of toxins which, somehow or other, had found their way from the products and chimneys of the chemical industry into the farthest, seemingly untouched corner of Nature. At the Rio Earth Summit of 1992 this experience of global ecological crisis gave rise to the political formula and demand for 'sustainable development'. Even if the actual interpretation of this principle differs from group to group around the world, and even if the follow-up conference in New York in 1997 confirmed how few practical consequences such summits usually have, there is now a yardstick (however contradictory and in need of political negotiation) with which to measure and criticize what all social players do everywhere in the world, in every domain from

consumption through production to architecture, transport, municipal politics, and so on. This is the yardstick of *ecological globalization*.

Financial jugglers   A few years ago, a young money-juggler whose
métier was half-permitted, half-forbidden transnational speculation managed to ruin a venerable old English bank by losing
close to a billion pounds in a trice. A new *virtual economy* has
sprung up in the jungle of the world market, and its money-
flows dissolve in a haze of data and information that are less and
less connected to any material substratum. The new speculative
dangers resulting from this escape the control of national states,
and indeed rob national economies of their foundations without
offering any framework for the regulation of transnational or global economies, of the process of *economic globalization*.

A Berlin–California airport announcement   It is ten o'clock in the
evening. At Berlin's Tegel Airport a slick-friendly voice informs
the weary passengers that their flight to Hamburg is ready for
boarding. The voice belongs to Angelika B., who is sitting in
front of a console in California – for after six p.m. Berlin time
Tegel's announcement service is provided online from California.
The reasons are as simple as they are understandable: in California,
no extra payment has to be made for late working because it is still
daytime; and indirect labour costs for the same activity are considerably lower than in Germany. Telecommunications have made
this possible by removing what used to seem an inescapable part of
the labour system of industrial society: that is, the need for people
to work together at a certain place to produce goods or services.
Jobs can now be exported, while employees 'cooperate' across
countries and continents or provide services through 'direct' contact with faraway recipients and consumers. In theory, then, just as
one could organize a world trip to experience springtime in every
continent, the labour and production processes could be distributed across the globe in such a way that the lowest wage was paid at
every hour of the day yet the requisite cooperation was always
secured. This would be globalized *labour cooperation* or *production*.

Khaled, king of rai   In February 1997 *Aïcha*, the latest hit by the
exiled Algerian 'rai king' Khaled, was selected as the best song of
the year in France. It was already remarkable that a song in praise
of an Arab girl should be playing on the turntables of all the main
French radio stations (not only of the Arabic pirate radios); it
meant that North African immigrants had been accepted into the

(pop) culture of the French nation. Seen from abroad, Khaled even represents France. His music captivates people in countries as different as Egypt, Israel and even conservative Saudi Arabia, with local versions coming out in Hebrew, Turkish and Hindi. Khaled plays his instrument against the West's Arabophobia. His person and his music prove that globalization does not have to be a one-way street, that regional musical cultures can acquire world stages and a global significance. This is *cultural globalization.*

Globalization has certainly been the most widely used – and mis-used – keyword in disputes of recent years and will be of the coming years too; but it is also one of the most rarely defined, the most nebulous and misunderstood, as well as the most politically effec-tive. As the above-mentioned cases show, it is necessary to distin-guish a number of *dimensions* of globalization: any list of these would have to include, without making any claim to completeness or rigour, the dimensions of *communications technology, ecology, econom-ics, work organization, culture* and *civil society.* Especially if we take the dimension that is nearly always at the centre of public debate – namely, economic globalization – the fog by no means clears. Is it a question of direct investment abroad by German firms, or of the international operations of large corporations? Is it *de*nationalization of the economy that is involved, and hence the fact that national brand-names are becoming as fictitious as national economies, so that the prosperity of a 'national' industry no longer coincides with the prosperity of (national) citizens? Are we talking of that 'virtual economy' of monetary and financial flows which appears detached from any material substratum of use-value production? Or is the real point the much more banal one that the German economy is under pressure from cheaper production elsewhere in the world?[1]

This last tendency is often overstressed, especially in Germany. For the facts do not really support any idea that globalization, in the sense of a transfer of jobs from Germany to countries with lower wage costs, is already a *fait accompli.* For a long time now, this form of globalization has *not* been a major cause of unemploy-ment.[2] It is true that, in some sectors, low-skill, low-pay jobs have been hard hit by competition from Eastern Europe or the Asian 'tiger states'. But such problems resulting from adjustments in the international division of labour affect only 10 per cent or so of jobs, and can hardly be projected onto the economy as a whole. Besides, German exports to these countries have also risen by above-aver-age amounts in recent years. A massive transfer of jobs, not offset by additional export demand, has not been demonstrated.[3] In fact, many speak in this context not of globalization but of *international-ization*, to underline that trade relations still mainly take place between highly industrialized countries *within* the great economic areas of Europe, America and the Pacific Basin.[4]

And then there is the truly thorny question of *when* globalization began. Many date the 'capitalist world-system' (Immanuel Waller-stein) back to the beginning of colonialism in the sixteenth century; others to the emergence of international corporations. Still others consider that globalization started with the ending of fixed exchange-rates or the collapse of the Eastern bloc...[5]

This may be why the concept and discourse of globalization are so fuzzy. To pin them down is like trying to nail a blancmange to the wall.

Is it not possible, however, to extract a common denominator from the various dimensions of globalization and the associated disputes? It is indeed. One constant feature is the overturning of the central premiss of the first modernity: namely, the idea that *we live and act in the self-enclosed spaces of national states and their respective national societies.* Globalization means that borders become mark-edly less relevant to everyday behaviour in the various dimensions of economics, information, ecology, technology, cross-cultural con-flict and civil society. It points to something not understood and hard to understand yet at the same time familiar, which is changing everyday life with considerable force and compelling everyone to adapt and respond in various ways. Money, technologies, commod-ities, information and toxins 'cross' frontiers as if they did not exist. Even things, people and ideas that governments would like to keep out (for example, drugs, illegal immigrants or criticisms of human rights abuses) find their way into new territories. So does globaliza-tion conjure away distance. It means that people are thrown into transnational lifestyles that they often neither want nor understand – or, following Anthony Giddens's definition, it means *acting and living (together) over distances, across the apparently separate worlds of national states, religions, regions and continents.*[6]

The overcoming of distance has the following consequences: 'The world's spatial matrix no longer contains any blank areas, and in principle it enables anyone to orient themselves regardless of the point on the globe at which they find themselves. Thanks to modern means of communication and transport, globalization is [...] in principle possible without any effort.' It is becoming a matter of everyday experience, of 'provincial behaviour', so to speak.

An odyssey or Robinson Crusoe's desert island are today unimagin-able artistic modes of perceiving the world, because heroes such as Odysseus or Crusoe would cut an absurd figure when German-American school exchanges are routine events and protests by European MPs against French nuclear tests are organized in a global sphere that Captain Cook would have had to spend a whole lifetime covering. [...] The many times in the many regions of the world are being drawn together into a single standardized and standardizing world-time, not only because the simultaneity of non-simultaneous events can be 'virtually' produced by modern media (so that any non-simultaneous, merely local or regional occurrence becomes part of world history), but also because synchronous simultaneity turns into diachronous non-simultaneity in such a way that artificial cause–effect chains can be generated. A 'temporally compact globe' is coming into being. Events from different parts of the world and with varying significance can now be relocated on a *single* temporal axis, instead of many different ones. [...] When the currency and stock exchanges open in Frankfurt, the closing rates in Tokyo, Singapore and Hong Kong are already known, and when the day begins in Wall Street dealers already know how rates have been shaping up on the European exchanges. Things are simpler still when foreign-exchange dealers are present twenty-four hours a day on the world's marketplaces, able to carry off the slightest arbitrage profits. [...] Economically, then, the earth is no longer big and wide and no longer has far and distant lands; it is dense and small and close, with (money) markets linked to one another by telecommunications. For the costs of overcoming space, and the time expenditure necessary to achieve it, are so small that they scarcely count.[7]

Globalization calls into question *a basic premiss of the first moder-nity*: the conceptual figure that A. D. Smith calls '*methodological nationalism*',[8] according to which the contours of society largely coincide with those of the national state. With multidimensional globalization, it is not only a new set of connections and cross-connections between states and societies which comes into being. Much more far-reaching is the breakdown of the basic assumptions whereby societies and states have been conceived, organized and experienced as *territorial units separated from one another*. Globality means that the unity of national state and national society comes unstuck; new relations of power and competition, conflict and intersection, take shape between, on the one hand, national states and actors, and on the other hand, transnational actors, identities, social spaces, situations and processes.

1

The World Horizon Opens Up: On the Sociology of Globalization

The bourgeoisie has through its exploitation of the world market given a cosmopolitan character to production and consumption in every country. To the great chagrin of reactionists, it has drawn from under the feet of industry the national ground on which it stood. All old-established national industries have been destroyed or are daily being destroyed. They are dislodged by new industries, whose introduction becomes a life and death question for all civilized nations. [...] In place of the old local and national seclusion and self-sufficiency, we have intercourse in every direction, universal interdependence of nations. And as in material, so also in intellectual production. The intellectual creations of individual nations become common property. National one-sidedness and narrow-mindedness become more and more impossible, and from the numerous national and local literatures, there arises a world literature.[1]

This quotation is not from some neoliberal manifesto of 1996 but from the *Communist Manifesto* of Marx and Engels, first published in February 1848. It shows a number of things: first, that the authors of the *Communist Manifesto* already eulogized the revolutionary role of the 'bourgeoisie' in world history; second, that the debate on 'exploitation of the world market' goes back much further than the short-term memory of public discussions would care to admit; third, that ironically the neoliberal and original Marxist positions share the same basic assumptions; and fourth, but not least, that the national vision which still holds the social sciences captive was already being questioned when it first emerged in the maelstrom of rising industrial capitalism.

Sociology as the power to create intellectual order: the container theory of society

'Modern' sociology is defined in its typical textbooks as the 'modern' science of 'modern' society. This both conceals and helps to gain acceptance for a classificatory schema that we might call the *container theory of society*.

1 According to this theory, societies both politically and theoretically presuppose 'state control of space' (J. Agnew and S. Corbridge), so that sociology here aligns itself with the regulatory authority or power of the national state. This is expressed in a vision of societies as (by definition) subordinate to states, of societies as *state* societies, of social order as state order. Thus, both in everyday life and in scientific discourse, one speaks of 'French', 'American' or 'German' society.

Furthermore, the concept of the political is associated not with society but with the state – which has not always been the case, as M. Viroli has shown.[2] Only in this conceptual and institutional framework do 'modern' societies become individual societies separate from one another. They really are held in the space controlled by national states *as in a container*. At the same time, it is part of the very concept of 'modern' societies that they are unpolitical, whereas political action is located only in the space controlled by the state.

2 This schema applies not only outwardly but also on the inside. The internal space of outwardly separable societies is subdivided into a number of totalities which, on the one hand, are conceptualized and analysed as *collective identities* (classes, status groups, religious and ethnic groups, male and female ways of living) and, on the other hand, are classified according to the organic 'social system' metaphor and theoretically inserted into the autonomous worlds of economics, politics, law, science, family, etc., each with its own distinctive 'logics' or 'codes'. Internal homogeneity is essentially a creation of state control. All kinds of social practices – production, culture, language, labour market, capital, education – are stamped and standardized, defined and rationalized, by the national state, but at least are labelled as national economy, national language, literature, public life, history, and so on. The state establishes a territorial unit as a 'container', in which

statistics are systematically collected about economic and social processes and situations. In this way, the categories of the state's self-observation become the categories of empirical social science, so that sociological definitions of reality confirm those of bureaucracy.

3 This image of externally and internally differentiated societies, constituted by individual national states, goes together with the *evolutionary self-image* and self-consciousness of modern societies. To be modern means to be superior. This universalist pretension is expressed, in the basic rights and rules of democratic self-regulation, as a claim to 'human emancipation from the self-incurred dependence of a minor' (Kant). But the claim to bestow happiness condensed, first, in the violent history of European colonialism and imperialism, and then, after the Second World War, in so-called 'development politics' and the 'theory of developing countries'. It is no accident that the word 'modernization' made its debut in the early fifties, in a book entitled *The Modernization of Developing Countries*. The empirical political and social sciences, seeing themselves as policy doctors or engineers, then worked out 'social indicators' that seemed to make it possible to measure the stages and successes of modernization and, in the case of national states, to monitor and shape the process.

I do not want to make a name for myself by setting up Aunt Sallies. Debates of recent years have severely shaken the axioms of a sociology of the first modernity focused on the national state. But its programmed vision – most of all in organized research and a number of long-standing controversies – remains dominant particularly in Germany. And what this container theory of society permits, or indeed compels, is a return to the origins of sociology in the formative period of the nation-state in nineteenth- and early twentieth-century Europe. The association between sociology and nation-state was so extensive that the image of 'modern', organized individual societies – which became definitive with the national model of political organization – itself became an absolutely necessary concept in and through the founding work of the classical social scientists. Beyond all their differences, such theorists as Émile Durkheim, Max Weber and even Karl Marx shared a territorial definition of modern society,[3] and thus a model of society centred on the national state, which has today been shaken by globality and globalization. If a Spenglerian mood of decline can be felt everywhere in people's musings, it surely has something to do with the fact that both society and sociology are caught in the 'territorial trap' (Agnew and Corbridge) of equating society with the national state. But the world is not declining, because – as Max Weber argued against himself, as it were – the light of the great cultural problems moves on and scientists too are forced to revise their thinking, to reorient themselves conceptually in the non-integrated multiplicity of a world without frontiers.

To make this background assumption clear and conscious, nothing is as helpful as to develop and probe *alternatives*. The sociology of globalization may be thought of as involving a loose, motley collection of dissidents from the sociology of national states. In comparison with the mainstream, it has long been a question of theories and research projects or approaches, often indeed no more than promises, which have arisen in quite different cultural and thematic contexts (from research into migration, through international class analysis, international politics and the theory of democracy, to cultural studies and the sociology of big cities), which often contradict one another, yet which somehow or other break through the thought-barrier of the national state – and, we should stress, do so less through criticism than through the working out of alternative ways of thinking. In other words, the globalization debate in the social sciences may be understood and developed as a fruitful dispute about which basic assumptions and images of society, which *units for analysis*, can *replace* the axiomatics of the national state.

Thought and research that remain trapped in a vision of separate social worlds organized on a national basis can find no place for anything that falls between the inner and the outer. This intermediate category – the category of the ambivalent, the mobile, the volatile, the Here-and-There – first opens up in the context of migration research, in the beginnings of *transnational social spaces*. World-system theory then deepens this perspective to the point that all social action is seen as taking place within *one overarching* framework, the framework of the capitalist world-system, in which an advancing inequality and division of labour install themselves.

But this world-system view has in turn been nuanced by reference to what the political theorist James Rosenau calls 'the two worlds of world politics': that is, the idea that there is not a single global society but at least *two* competing ones: the society of (national) states, and the many different transnational organizations, players, groups and individuals who build and consolidate a tissue of social relationships.

In all the analyses mentioned so far, spaces of transnational action arise in one way or another because actors set out to achieve them. In the theory of *world risk society*, however, the category of unintended consequences appears in place of the basic unity of purposive action. It is global risks (their social and political construction), and thus various ecological crises (or definitions of crisis), which bring about new kinds of world disorder and turmoil.

In research associated with 'cultural theory', the linearity assumption and the Either-Or of national axiomatics are replaced by Both-And postulates: globalization *and* regionalization, linkage *and* fragmentation, centralization *and* decentralization, are dynamics that belong together as two sides of the same coin.

In considerations on *transnational civil society*, socio-cultural processes, experiences, conflicts and identities become visible which orient themselves by a 'one-world model' of transnational social movements, globalization 'from below', and a new world citizenship. Here the axiomatics that equates modernity with non-political individual societies breaks down. World society without a world state means a society that is *not politically organized*, where new opportunities for action and power arise for transnational actors that have no democratic legitimation. This means that a new transnational space of the moral and the subpolitical is opening up, as we may see in such phenomena as consumer boycotts but also in questions to do with cross-cultural communication and criticism.

These basic ideas associated with post-national or transnational images of society, and the units that they mark out for investigation, should now be briefly outlined. At the same time, 'development logics' will have to be contrasted with the dynamic of globalization, so that a complex picture (one which includes internal contradictions) is drawn of the globalization debate in the social sciences.

Transnational social spaces

The pill to be used against abstractness, including the abstractness of 'the global', is examples. What does 'transnational social space' mean?

Africa is not a continent but a concept

As Patricia Alleyne-Dettmers shows in her study 'Tribal Arts', Africa is not a fixed geographical magnitude, not a separate place on the globe, but a *transnational idea and the staging of that idea.*[4] This is intentionally organized at many different places in the world: in the Caribbean, in the ghettoes of Manhattan, in the Southern states of the USA, in the *favelas* of Brazil, but also at Europe's largest street carnival in London. Here the masks, music, costumes and dance are carefully selected and designed in accordance with two governing principles. Everything is drawn from the 'African' reservoir of cultural ideas anywhere in the world; and everything must also be adapted to the subcultural peculiarities of London's black districts.

Nothing in the whole of the African continent corresponds to the Africa that is staged on the streets of London. How could it? Where is Africa to be found in a world society with porous frontiers? In the ruins that the colonial masters have left behind in Africa? In the big-city shapes of an only half-modernized Africa? In the African four-star hotels? On organized safaris? In the 'back to the roots' hopes and illusions of Black Americans? In the books about Africa that are written in Western universities? In the Caribbean with its riotous profusion of forms? Or even in the struggle for a national identity in Britain's black subcultures?

In the eyes of those who design the dances and masks of Notting Hill's 'African carnival', Africa has lost its geographical location. For them 'Africa' is a vision, an idea, from which models can be derived for a *black aesthetic*. Not the least aim of this is to ground, create or renew an African national identity for blacks *in Britain*. This Africa, or counter-Africa, is in the strictest sense an 'imagined community'; it serves to break down and overcome the alienation of Afro-Caribbean groups in Britain. We could say that 'there is Africa' in Notting Hill.

Transnational 'communities' really are that paradoxical. What is 'discovered' here, but in reality *invented*, often contradicts what floats around as 'Africa' in the heads of each transnational 'African'. A large part of historical Africa was reduced to slavery and scattered around the world. Its cultures were broken up and destroyed. Hence those people who are called 'African' (often by others) have also shaken off that image of Africa. For many 'Africans', indeed, Africa and being African is the very identity they oppose and reject. Perhaps they grew up in a pot-pourri of cultures where any clarity about the matter had long been lost, and where the quality of being black had an especially negative value. At any event, the outcome is quite paradoxical. Blacks in the Caribbean and in English cities associate 'Africa' with *non*-identity and *non*-progress, with drums, dancing, superstition, naked, uneducated tribesmen, permanent hopelessness.

One can see in this the negative mirror image of a Eurocentric idea of Africa, which blacks have adopted in the Western metropolis. But this only makes the question sharper: what and where is 'Africa' within transnational social space?

American Mexicans and Mexican Americans

Transnational social spaces cancel the local associations of community that are contained in the national concept of society. The figure of thought at issue joins together what cannot be combined: to live and act both here and there. Ludger Pries has illustrated what this means from the field of migration research.[5]

In the imaginative and political world of individual societies organized as national states, migration is broken down into the stages and contexts of dissolution, travel, arrival and (not necessarily successful) integration, each of which requires separate causal investigation. By contrast, the approach centred on transnational social spaces maintains that something new is emerging: social contexts of life and action to which Here-and-There or Both-And applies. Between the separate, organized worlds, what Martin Albrow calls new 'social landscapes' combine and transmute places of departure *and* places of arrival.

In a study of transnational forms of community, life and politics stretching between Mexicans in North America and their places of origin, Robert Smith shows how this everyday link operates.

> For some communities of the *Mixteca Poblana*, support committees were organized in New York that collected money among migrant workers for the laying of drinking-water pipes in their community of origin, or for the restoration of churches and village squares. Major decisions and issues were sorted out in tele-conferences with officials in the community of origin. It was not uncommon for the sums of money collected in New York to be greater than the public spending on infrastructure in the Mexican community. One important aspect – and a serious argument for the stability and

stabilization of *transnational social spaces* – is the fact that the Mexican state has now recognized not only the huge economic significance of the migrant workers, but also their political significance. Since the presidential elections of 1988, the critical voting power of the Mexican workers abroad (who voted in an above-average proportion for the ruling PRI party) has become especially apparent, and the Mexican government pursues an active policy of integrating them economically, politically and culturally. Thus, Mexican mayors sometimes travel to New York to put investment proposals for village development before migrant associations. And the Embassy actively supports migrants' sports associations, as well as the development of Guadalupe groups (which are supposed to organize the cult worship of the Virgin of Guadalupe, the main national holy figure in Mexico). At every level of Mexican politics, labour migration is no longer seen just as a (passive) safety-valve for employment problems, but as an important capital and human resource for the country's own economic and social development. As a result of this policy orientation, the Mexico–USA migration system increasingly involves institutional pillars that give a flanking stability to the emergent *transnational social spaces*. [...] The social and economic dovetailing between region of origin and region of arrival is not, however, just a matter of nostalgia or tradition (sticking to village festivals) or of care for an older generation that has stayed behind. Rather, what develop in the *Mixteca* are economic activities that point far beyond purely transitory relations of a migratory character. In Greater New York, for example, there are a *Puebla Food Incorporation* and a clan of tortilla-producing families that has already made millions from the traditional Mexican food. Transnational production and marketing structures thus stretch between the *Mixteca* and New York – structures that imply a dimension of 'cumulative causation'. Insofar as the dynamic of migration networks keeps the migratory flow moving, the demand increases for specifically Mexican foods and services, which in turn open up new opportunities for migration-related gain in the regions of origin and arrival. [...]

In New York itself, for example, newly arriving migrant workers can turn not only to relatives and acquaintances, but also to a well-polished network of informal support groups, specialist services and solidarity organizations (legal advice bureaux, committees to help people from special ethnic groups or regions, etc.). Whole streets (e.g. the northern part of Amsterdam Street, or certain neighbourhoods in Queen's) bear witness to this by now very stable infrastructure, on which transnational migrants can build and which is at the same time reproduced by them. There are gainful activities and social groups (of Mexicans and US-Americans) which live entirely on the constant migration and *transmigrants*, and whose vital interest lies in further building up *transnational social spaces*. This also applies to the sports associations, where some of the migrant workers living in New York (perhaps *indocumentados*, without a work or residence permit) come together every Sunday. In the 1996 football season, sixty-five teams were registered for the Mexicans' own league. [...]

In the USA (so far more strongly in California than in New York, for example), various political groupings and organizations (e.g. the *Frente indígena oaxaqueña binacional* or the newspaper *La Mixteca Año 2000*) support the economic interests and human rights of the migrant workers. The political pressure these groups can exert within the USA, but above all on the Mexican side of the border, is quite often greater than the potential influence of local politicians. The director of the Mexican football league in New York put it like this: 'As simple Mexicans and migrant workers, we don't count for anything at all. But now we're suddenly being courted by high-up Mexican politicians.'[6]

To the best of my knowledge, no one has yet investigated whether – as one may suspect – similar transnational social spaces exist between Turkish Germans and German Turks.

Logics, dimensions and consequences of globalization

As we have already intimated, a basic dispute runs like a red thread through the globalization literature.[7] The question of the impetus behind globalization finds two contrasting answers (each in turn taking a number of different forms). The first group of authors point to the existence of one dominant 'logic' of globalization, while others work with theories that suggest a phenomenon with a complex set of causes. This central theoretical controversy, by the way, entails that the word 'globalization' does not have a single horizon of meaning, that indeed often *contradictory* meanings are associated with it.

At the same time, we see the sociology of globalization repeating the historical divergence between Marx and Weber: that is, between a view of the dominance of the economic, and a theoretical pluralism involving economic, social and cultural approaches (and for which any analysis that operates with just a single logic therefore excludes a crucial dimension of globalization). The adding together of (apparently) mutually exclusive logics of globalization introduces, or slides into, a view in which different partial logics of globalization compete with one another.

First, we should consider approaches which hold one special dimension or logic of globalization to be central. Here the key authors are Wallerstein, Rosenau, Gilpin, Held, Robertson and Appadurai, in addition to Giddens as the common reference point. Wallerstein – one of the first in the seventies to confront the social sciences with the question of globalization – introduced the concept of a *world-system* and argued that capitalism was the engine of globalization. Rosenau, Gilpin and Held have concerned themselves more with international politics. They challenge the nation-state orthodoxy by stressing the importance both of technological globalization (the science and information society) and of political-military factors and viewpoints (power politics).

No doubt, the ecological crisis and – following the Rio conference in 1992 – its worldwide recognition have had a lasting and devastating impact on ways of thinking and acting that focus on the national state. World society, accused of being a 'world *risk* society', has become conscious of itself as sharing a common ecological fate.

Robertson, Appadurai, Albrow, Featherstone, Lash, Urry and many others argue within the tradition of cultural theory. Strongly opposing the widespread notion of a 'McDonaldization' of the planet, they insist that *cultural* globalization does not mean the world is becoming culturally homogeneous. Rather, it involves a process of 'glocalization', which is highly contradictory both in content and in its multiple consequences. Two of the most problematic effects for the stratification of world society should be briefly examined: the problem of *global wealth, local poverty* (Bauman), and the problem of *capitalism without work*.

Each of the authors mentioned locates the origin and results of the globalization dynamic mainly in *one* sector of institutional action (whether the economy, technology, international politics, ecology, culture or world industry), or else in new social inequalities measured on a world scale. It is in the interplay of these perspectives that a plural sociology of globalization comes into view.

Capitalist world-system: Wallerstein

The conception of transnational social spaces is a medium-range theory. It breaks down the nation-state view of society and its 'container theory' of nationally separate social worlds, replacing them with *different* modes of life, transnationally integrated spaces of social action that circumvent or cross over postulated frontiers.

The metaphor of a space or area is here contradictory. For the dominant feature of the 'spaces' in question is that they *overcome* distance. 'Transnational' implies that forms of life and action emerge whose inner logic comes from the inventiveness with which people create and maintain social lifeworlds and action contexts where distance is not a factor. This raises a number of questions for sociological research. How are transnational life-worlds transcending distance and frontiers *possible* in the first place? How can they be put together and cultivated at the level of individual action, often in the teeth of resistance from national state bureaucracies? Are they stateless, or perhaps even institution-less, early forms of transnational world societies? Which orientations, resources and institutions favour or hinder them? What political consequences (disintegration or transnational mobilization) are associated with them?

What is clear is that, in these transnational social landscapes, something is (often illegally) blended together which seriously hinders national states in their claim to exercise control and order. The spaces for living and acting which take shape here are *'impure'*. To analyse them, sociology must stop thinking in Either-Or terms and open itself to specific, *distinguishable* modes of Both-And living.

Wallerstein's radical move replaces the image of separate individual societies with one of a *world-system* in which *everything* – every society, every government, every company, every culture, every class, every household, every individual – must insert and assert itself within a single division of labour. This single world-system, which provides a framework for the measurement of social inequalities on a world scale, imposes itself with the rise of capitalism. For Wallerstein, then, the very logic of capitalism is necessarily global.

Once it had arisen in Europe in the sixteenth century, the capitalist dynamic took hold of, and thoroughly transformed, more and more 'continents', spaces and niches of social life. 'The whole planet operates within this regulatory mechanism of a *binding* and *constant* division of labour, which we call the capitalist world economy.'[8]

According to Wallerstein, a capitalist world economy has three basic elements. First, metaphorically speaking, it consists of a single market governed by the principle of profit maximization. Second, it has a series of state structures whose power varies both internally and externally; these state structures chiefly serve to 'hinder' the 'free' functioning of the capitalist market, in order to 'improve' the prospective profits of one or more groups. Third, in a capitalist world economy, the appropriation of surplus labour takes place within a relationship of exploitation not between two classes but among three layers: the *central areas or heartlands,* the *semiperiphery* and the *peripheral countries and regions.* (The question of which countries or regions belong where, and by which criteria, triggers historical-empirical disputes that are hard to resolve.)

Thus, while European capitalism since the collapse of the Eastern bloc has been forming a universal economic space or world market, humanity has remained divided into national states and identities, each with its own conceptions of sovereignty and descendance. At the same time, conflicts are multiplying and intensifying within the world-system, because it produces not only fabulous riches but also terrible poverty. The patterns of global inequality follow the tripartite division of social space into centre, semiperiphery and periphery – a division that integrates the world-system upon a conflictual basis.

Periodically occurring crises lead, in Wallerstein's view, to restructuring which intensifies the division of power and inequality and increases the level of conflict within the world-system. The universalization and deepening of the capitalist logic engenders resistance on a world scale, which includes anti-Western, anti-modern, fundamentalist reactions, as well as the environmental movement or neo-nationalist currents. The inner logic of the capitalist world-system thus engenders both world integration and world decomposition. The question of whether there is a positive side to all this is given no answer. For Wallerstein, the world-system is in the end threatened with collapse.

This line of argument (which we have only been able to outline here) has two striking features: it is both monocausal and economic. Globalization is exclusively defined in terms of institutionalization of the world market.

However, at least three points may be made in criticism of this approach. First, there are obvious difficulties in specifying and testing the historical-empirical content of the theory. Second, globalization is said to have begun with Columbus's discovery and subjugation of the New World, and is thus anything but specific to the late twentieth century. This means that Wallerstein's proposed framework does not enable us to identify what is historically new about the transnational.

Third, for all the dialectics, Wallerstein's is a *linear* argument. It never really considers whether the world market, as Marx and Engels argued in the *Communist Manifesto*, inconspicuously and inadvertently produces *cosmopolitan* conflicts and identities.[9]

— Post-international politics: Rosenau, Gilpin, Held —

Rosenau, too, breaks with nationally centred thinking. But he does not replace the anarchy of national states with a world system of the world market; instead, he distinguishes between two phases of international politics. In his schema, globalization means that humanity has left behind the age when national states dominated, or monopolized, the international scene. Now an age of *post-international politics* has begun, in which national players have to share the global arena and global power with international organizations, transnational concerns and transnational social and political movements. Empirically, this may be seen *inter alia* in the sheer number of international organizations, including NGOs such as Greenpeace, which is evidently still increasing.

Asked whether it was wrong to think that US foreign policy was striking out in new directions, Secretary of State Timothy Wirth replied:

> The maxim 'Think globally, act locally!' is clearly becoming a reality. We see how international institutions and resolutions are becoming more and more important. There is a growing feeling that nations can also be governed by international institutions, and not just at a national level. The foreign policy establishment is starting to think in different dimensions from those of military and economic power, rifle bullets and dollars. Now there are also global problems such as worldwide human rights and refugee programmes, or containing corruption and environmental disasters. This globality changes our thinking.

And this is how he sees the role of citizens and action groups in relation to globalization:

> Alongside internationalization, the growing influence of grassroots initiatives is the second challenge to the previous conception of politics. There is huge pressure for a decentralization of politics, already coming from the new possibilities of communication. Fax

and the Internet are more and more part of everyday life. Anyone can talk to anyone at lightning speed, all over the world, without having to rely on government channels or diplomats.[10]

For Rosenau, then, the passage from the national to the postnational age has to do, first, with conditions within the international political system and, second, with the fact that the monocentric power structure of rival national states has been and is being replaced by a polycentric distribution of power in which a great variety of transnational and national actors compete or cooperate with one another.

There are thus two arenas of world society: a *community of states*, in which the rules of diplomacy and national power remain the key variables; and a world of *transnational subpolitics*, in which such diverse players as multinational corporations, Greenpeace and Amnesty International, but also the World Bank, NATO or the European Union, stride around.

Polycentric world politics The opposition between world-system theory and this view of a *dual* world society is obvious enough. In place of a single world-market system 'governed' by economics, Rosenau postulates a *polycentric world politics* in which it is not only capital or national governments, nor even the UN, World Bank or Greenpeace, which have the only say, but *all* compete with one another to achieve their aims – even if they do not all have the same power opportunities.

Rosenau also differs from Wallerstein in seeing the *technological* dimension and dynamic of globalization as the root of the passage from a politics dominated by national states to a polycentric politics. His theoretical political studies have taught him again and again that international ties of dependence have acquired a new density and significance. The reason for this, in his view, is the enormous and still continuing upsurge of information and communications technology.

> It is technology that has so greatly diminished geographical and social distances through the jet-powered airliner, the computer, the orbiting satellite, and the many other inventions that now move people, ideas, and goods more rapidly and surely across space and time than ever before. [...] It is technology, in short, that has fostered an interdependence of local, national, and international communities that is far greater than any previously experienced.[11]

Rosenau's argument thus combines two factors: the advent of the information and science society, and its overcoming of distance and frontiers as a result of the multiplication of transnational players and organizations. This *irreversibly polycentric world politics* defines a situation where:[12]

- *transnational organizations* such as the World Bank, the Catholic Church, the International Association of Sociologists, McDonald's, Volkswagen, drug cartels and the Italian mafia, as well as the new International of NGOs, act alongside, with or against one another;
- *transnational problems* such as climate change, drugs, AIDS, ethnic conflicts and currency crises determine the political agenda;
- *transnational events* such as the World Cup, the Gulf War, the American election campaign or the publication of a Salman Rushdie novel can lead via satellite television to turmoil in quite different countries and continents;
- *transnational 'communities'* develop, for example, around religion (Islam), knowledge (experts), lifestyles (pop, ecology), kinship (the family) or political orientations (environmental movement, consumer boycotts); and
- *transnational structures* such as various forms of work, production and cooperation, banks, financial flows, technical knowledge, and so on, create and stabilize across distances the contexts of action and crisis.

Gilpin's approach to globalization, on the other hand, remains sceptical about all the talk of novelty and takes a position close to the orthodox view of international politics, arguing, as it were, on the basis of its inner logic. Gilpin sees that national states are more than ever linked – not to say, shackled – to one another. Unlike Wallerstein and Rosenau, however, he stresses that globalization comes about only under certain conditions of international politics, that it is the product of a *'permissive'* global order. By this he means an order among states which alone makes it possible for dependence and relationship networks to be established and maintained beyond and among national authorities.

Globalization, understood as the expansion of transnational spaces and actors, is in this view paradoxically still dependent upon national authorities or, to be more precise, upon a *hegemonic power*. Globalization, so to speak, presupposes the tacit *consent* of

national states. The openness, or 'permissiveness', which is necessary for the development of a world market, world churches,
world corporations, world banks and worldwide NGOs can survive and spread only in the shadow of a matching concentration of
state power.

In Gilpin's approach, then, which asserts the primacy of national
politics over all other factors, globalization is necessarily *contingent*
and under threat, in the sense that the emergence and development
of transnational social spaces and players presupposes a hegemonic power structure and an international political regime. Only this
can, if need be, guarantee the openness of the world order.

> My position is that a hegemon is necessary to the existence of a
> liberal international economy. [...] historical experience suggests
> that, in the absence of a dominant liberal power, international eco-
> nomic cooperation has been extremely difficult to attain or sustain
> and conflict has been the norm. [...] The expansion and success of
> the market in integrating modern economic life could not have
> occurred without the favourable political environment provided by
> the liberal economic power.[13]

Sovereignty divided and shackled   Against the theory of a hegemonic
power structure as the precondition of globalization, it can and
must be objected that globalization is making obsolete the concept
of political sovereignty upon which it is based. This is the argument put forward by David Held. He shows how – as a result of
international treaties, the internationalization of political decision-
making and the growing interdependence of security policy
(including the now far-advanced internationalization of arms production), as well as through the arms trade and the international
division of labour – national politics has been losing what used to
be the core of its power: namely, its sovereignty.

In the wake of globalization, Held writes,

> the 'disjunctures' reveal a set of forces which combine to restrict the
> freedom of action of governments and states by blurring the bound-
> aries of domestic politics, transforming the conditions of political
> decision-making, changing the institutional and organizational con-
> text of national polities, altering the legal framework and adminis-
> trative practices of governments and obscuring the lines of
> responsibility and accountability of national states themselves.
> These processes alone warrant the statement that the operation of
> states in an ever more complex international system both limits their

autonomy (in some spheres radically) and impinges increasingly upon their sovereignty. Any conception of sovereignty which interprets it as an illimitable and indivisible form of public power – entrenched securely in individual nation-states – is undermined. Sovereignty itself has to be conceived today as already divided among a number of agencies – national, regional and international – and limited by the very nature of this plurality.[14]

World risk society: economic globalization as forced politicization

Someone investigating the political implications of the new perception of ecological crisis will certainly encounter a wide range of answers. One of these will refer to a threat to civilization which cannot be attributed to any god, idols or nature but only to human decisions and the triumphs of industry, or indeed to the very claim of human civilization to shape and control the world. The other side of this is a sense of the *fragility* of civilization, which – to put it politically – can be produced by the experience of a common destiny. The word 'destiny' is appropriate here, because *everyone* may in principle be faced with the consequences of scientific-industrial decisions; but it is also inappropriate, because the impending threats are the result of human decision.

The ecological shock, then, has forcibly thrust upon people an experience which political theorists thought was the preserve of wars. However, there is a characteristic openness in this experience. The community of national history was always raised in the dialectic of enemy-images, and the awareness of ecological crisis may also vent itself in hysterical panic attacks directed against certain groups or things. Nevertheless, the fact that the threat knows no frontiers may mean that for the first time people will experience the common character of a destiny. Paradoxical as it may seem, it is arousing a *cosmopolitan* everyday consciousness which transcends even the borders between man, animal and plant. Threats create society, and global threats create global society. Nor is this all that justifies us in speaking of world risk society.[15]

The very different ways in which all the previously mentioned authors deploy the concept of a post-national social reality have one essential point in common: they all start from the premiss that transnational social spaces emerge only as a result of deliberate action; or, to put it less strongly, they assume the existence of purposive actors and institutions. The theory of world risk society, by contrast, does not make this assumption. It maintains that it is no longer possible to externalize the side-effects and dangers of highly developed industrial societies; that the associated risk-conflicts place a question mark over the whole institutional structure. It will be further argued below that transnational social spaces also come about conflictually and mysteriously through *un*intended, *denied* or *'repressed'* threats, 'behind people's backs', as it were.

This view appears to run straight up against the objection that unintended consequences must be known if they are to have any political effect. This cannot be denied. Yet the political, economic and cultural turmoil of world risk society can be understood only if one recognizes that publicly discussed dangers constitute a kind of 'negative currency'. They are coins that no one wants, but which find their way in nevertheless, compel people's attention, confuse and subvert. They turn upside down precisely what appeared to be solidly anchored in everyday normality.

One has only to think of the tragicomedy of mad cow disease in Europe. In the summer of 1997 in Upper Bavaria – a region protected from the supposedly British source of the danger by several frontiers and promises of police action – a visitor could drop into a pub-restaurant, open the menu and see a smiling local farmer in cosy harmony with his cattle and children. This photograph, and the advice that the steak of one's fancy would come from the cow in the picture, were supposed to restore the confidence that the ubiquitous reports of 'British' mad cow disease had shattered.

Three kinds of global threat may be distinguished. First, there are conflicts over the 'bad' other side of various 'goods': that is, ecological destruction and technological-industrial dangers *caused by affluence* (the ozone hole and greenhouse effect, but also the unpredictable and incalculable consequences of genetic engineering and reproductive medicine).

Second, there are ecological destruction and technological-industrial dangers *caused by poverty*. The Brundtland Commission was the first to point out, in 1987, that environmental destruction was not only the dangerous shadow of modern growth but also its exact opposite, because it was closely correlated with poverty. 'Inequality is the earth's most important "environmental" problem,' it stated, 'as well as its most important "development" problem.' From an integrated analysis of population and nutrition, loss of species and genetic resources, energy, industry and human settlement, it follows that all these things are interrelated and cannot be treated separately from one another.

'However,' writes Michael Zürn,

> there is a crucial difference between environmental destruction as a result of prosperity and environmental destruction as a result of poverty. Whereas many ecological dangers caused by affluence are the result of an externalization of production costs, ecological destruction caused by poverty involves self-destruction of the poor that also has side-effects for the rich. In other words, environmental destruction caused by affluence is distributed evenly across the globe, whereas environmental destruction caused by poverty mainly occurs at a certain time and place and only becomes international in the form of medium-term side-effects.[16]

The best-known example of this is the depletion of the tropical rainforest, currently running at a rate of some 17 million hectares per annum. Other examples are toxic waste (including waste imported from other countries) and obsolete large-scale technologies (e.g. in the chemical or atomic industry), and in future also genetic engineering and related research. These dangers result from a context of modernization processes begun but not completed. Industries develop with the potential to endanger the environment and life, but individual countries lack the institutional and political means to ward off the threat of destruction.

The dangers caused by either affluence or poverty are what might be called dangers of 'normality', which are constantly brought into the world through a lack of adequate safety provisions. Another, *third* type of danger comes from *weapons of mass destruction* (ABC weapons) – that is, from their possible use in the exceptional situation of war, not just from their deterrent capacity. Even after the end of the East–West conflict, the dangers of regional or global self-destruction by nuclear, chemical or biological weapons have by no means disappeared; indeed, they have broken out of the control structure of a superpower 'atomic pact'.

The dangers of military confrontation between states are compounded by the newly emerging dangers of fundamentalist or private *terrorism*. Less and less can it be ruled out that weapons of mass destruction, available not only to states but also to private organizations as a means of exerting (political) threats, will become a new source of danger in world risk society.

These various global dangers can and will complement and intensify one another. We must therefore now consider the inter-action between ecological destruction, wars and the effects of incomplete modernization.

In what ways does ecological destruction favour war – whether in the form of armed conflict over resources necessary to survival (water, for instance), or in the calls of ecological fundamentalists in the West for military intervention to halt such processes as the loss of tropical rainforest?

It is easy to imagine that a country living in ever greater poverty will exploit its environment to the hilt. In desperation (or as a way of politically concealing desperation), armed force may even be used to make a grab for resources that are necessary to another people's survival. Ecological devastation (for example, floods in Bangladesh) may trigger mass migration which then leads in turn to military conflict. Or else, states threatened with military defeat in a war may, as a 'last resort', try to destroy both their own and other countries' atomic or chemical installations, thereby threaten-ing nearby regions and cities with destruction. There are no limits to the nightmare scenarios of how the various dangers could all come together. Zürn speaks of a 'spiral of destruction', through which all such phenomena could culminate in one huge, overarch-ing crisis.

It is precisely this which the diagnosis of a world risk society is meant to address. The various global dangers cause cracks to appear in the pillars that have supported traditional security cal-culations. The potential damages are no longer limited in space and time: they are global and enduring; and it is hardly possible any longer to assign a clear-cut primary responsibility. Nor can loss or damage be financially compensated any longer, and there is no point in insuring oneself against the worst-case effects of the spiralling global dangers. There are not even any plans for after-care, should the worst case actually come to pass.

In this light, it is already clear that there are no global dangers per se, that they are indistinguishably mixed in with the poverty, ethnicity and nationality conflicts which have afflicted the world especially since the end of the order bound up with the East–West conflict. Thus, in the post-Soviet republics, a blunt diagnosis of environmental destruction is linked to political criticism of the imperial use of natural resources. To talk of one's 'native soil' is thus to claim rights both to natural resources *and* to national sovereignty.

The concept of world risk society may tempt one to exaggerate the independence of ecological crises, within a monocausal and one-dimensional view of global society. It is all the more necessary, therefore, to stress the special kind of *involuntary politicization* that risk conflicts bring about in all fields of social activity.

Perceived dangers appear to prise open firmly bolted mechanisms of social decision-making. Things which used to be negotiated and decided by managers and academics, behind closed doors and with no attempt at justification, must now suddenly have their consequences justified in the biting wind of public debate. Whereas the execution of particular legislation once seemed to take place automatically, those responsible now appear in public and, when the pressure is on, may even admit to mistakes or mention the alternatives that were once rejected. In sum, the risk technocracy unintentionally produces a political antidote as a result of, and in opposition to, its own way of handling things. Dangers which become publicly known, even though the relevant authorities claim to have everything under control, create new leeway for political action.[17]

Why the thesis of a McDonaldization of the world is wrong: paradoxes of cultural globalization

Kevin Robins has argued that the development of the world market has far-reaching consequences for cultures, identities and lifestyles.[18] The globalization of economic activity is accompanied by waves of cultural transformation, by a process that is called 'cultural globalization'. Centrally involved here, of course, is also the manufacturing of cultural symbols – a process which, to be sure, has long been observable. Both in the social sciences and among the wider public, a number of writers have adopted what may be called the *convergence of global culture* thesis. The keyword here has become *McDonaldization*. According to this view, there is an ever greater uniformity of lifestyles, cultural symbols and transnational modes of behaviour. In the villages of Lower Bavaria, just as in Calcutta, Singapore or the *favelas* of Rio de Janeiro, people watch *Dallas* on TV, wear blue jeans and smoke Marlboro as a sign of 'free, untouched nature'. In short, a global culture industry increasingly signifies the *convergence* of cultural symbols and ways of life.

The chairman of Euro-Disneyland puts it like this: 'Disney's characters are universal. You try and convince an Italian child that Topolino – the Italian name for Mickey Mouse – is American! Obviously you would stand no chance.'[19]

In this perspective, a negative utopia lies at the root of world market discourse. As the last niches are integrated into the world market, what emerges is indeed *one world*: not as a recognition of multiplicity or mutual openness, where images both of oneself and of foreigners are pluralist and cosmopolitan, but on the contrary as *a single commodity-world* where local cultures and identities are uprooted and replaced with symbols from the publicity and image departments of multinational corporations.

People are what they buy, or are able to buy. According to the argument we are considering, this law of cultural globalization continues to apply even when purchasing power is close to zero. Where purchasing power ends so too does *social* humanity – and the threat of exclusion begins. Exclusion! This is the sentence passed on those who fall outside the 'being equals design' equation.

The giant corporations, which aim at market-governed production of universal cultural symbols, employ in their own way the open-frontier world of information technologies about which Rosenau, for instance, goes into such raptures. Satellites make it possible to overcome all national and class boundaries, to plant the carefully devised glitter of white America in the hearts of people all around the world. The logic of economic activity does the rest.

Globalization, understood and forced through as an economic process, minimizes costs and maximizes profits. Even small market segments, with their corresponding lifestyles and consumption habits, can expect to win the applause of Wall Street once the barriers of oceans and continents fall away. Transregional market planning is thus a magic formula in the publicity and management departments of global culture industries. Although costs rise in the production of universally serviceable symbols, globalization offers itself as a promising route to the profit-paradise just around the corner.

'A cultural and social revolution is taking place as a result of economic globalization,' says a CNN spokesman. 'Employees in America are as much affected by this as the man in the street in Moscow or a manager in Tokyo. This means that what we do in and for America goes for everywhere in the world. Our news is global news.'

No more free, non-conformist information?   On the world information markets, a new gold-digging mood has been unleashing
powerful movements of corporate concentration. Observers see in
this the beginning of the end for free, non-conformist information.
And who with eyes to see could simply brush this fear aside?
    'A global information structure covers the earth like a spider's
web,' writes Ignacio Ramonet.

> It uses the advantages of digitalization and fosters the networking of
> all communication services. In particular, it promotes the link-up of
> three fields of technology – computers, telephones and television –
> which come together in multimedia and the Internet. There are 1.26
> billion television viewers around the world (more than 200 million
> connected to cable and some 60 million with digital television); there
> are 690 million telephone subscribers (including 80 million in mobile
> networks) and some 200 million computers (some 30 million of them
> connected to the Internet). It is predicted that by the year 2001 there
> will be more connections via the Internet than by telephone, that the
> number of Internet users will be between 600 million and one
> billion, and that the World Wide Web will comprise more than
> 100,000 commercial sites. The turnover of the communications
> industry, which in 1995 totalled roughly 1,000 billion dollars,
> might double in five years to account for some 10 per cent of the
> world economy. The computer, telephone and television giants
> know that in future profits will be made in the newly opened
> 'mines', where digital technology is being opened up before their
> fascinated, hungry eyes. At the same time, they realize that their
> territory will no longer be protected, that giants in neighbouring
> sectors are watching them with covetous glances. Ruthless warfare
> is the norm in the media sector. Those who used to specialize only in
> telephones now want to make television too, and vice versa. All
> companies involved in networking, especially those which maintain
> a supply network (electricity, telephone, water, gas, railways, motor-
> ways, etc.), are in a gold-digging mood and trying to secure their
> share of the multimedia cake. These rivals do battle with one
> another in every part of the globe. The names of these giant firms,
> the new world rulers, are: AT&T (the world-market leader in tele-
> phones), the duo formed by MCI (America's second-largest tele-
> phone network) and British Telecom, Sprint (the third-largest long-
> distance network inside the United States), Cable & Wireless (which
> controls Hong Kong Telecom, among others), Bell Atlantic, Nynex,
> US-West, TCI (the main cable television supplier), NTT (Japan's
> largest telephone company), Disney (which has now bought up

ABC), Time Warner (which belongs to CNN), News Corp., IBM, Microsoft (the number one in software), Netscape, Intel, and so on. [...] The higher logic of this shift in capitalism is not a quest for allies but the takeover of other companies. The aim, in a market characterized by constant and unpredictable technological acceleration and surprising consumer successes (such as the Internet boom), is to gain the know-how of those who have already established themselves in the market. [...] But if the newly acquired infrastructure is to be of real use to users, it must be possible for communications to circulate around the world without hindrance, as freely as the wind wafts over the oceans. This is the reason why the United States (the number-one producer of new technologies and the site of the major firms) has brought its full weight to bear in the pursuit of deregulation and economic globalization, so that as many countries as possible will open their borders to the 'free flow of information' – that is, to the giants of the US media and entertainment industry.[20]

Hawaii veal sausage: the new importance of the local And yet *Le Monde diplomatique*, from which this quotation is taken, is living proof against the pitch-black view that the media are threatened with a new, economically driven system of world rule. For that outspoken left-wing monthly also makes skilful use of the world information market: it now appears in several languages and – against the trend in the printed media – may have more than doubled its circulation over the past few years (even if the circulation of the French original has fallen to around 100,000 over the same period, with a resulting loss of advertising income).

The widespread view of a linear convergence of content and information driven by world-market concentration fails to appreciate the *paradoxes* and *ambivalences* – or, in old-fashioned terms, the *dialectic* – of globalization which cultural theory has theoretically identified and empirically investigated. Roland Robertson, one of the founders of cultural globalization theory and research, never tires of emphasizing that globalization always also involves a process of *localization*. Those working in the field of 'cultural studies' do reject the image of closed societies, each with its own cultural space, and think instead in terms of an immanent 'dialectical' process of cultural 'globalization', in which the opposite at the same time becomes both *possible* and *actual*. Their basic insight is that globalization does not mean globalization automatically, unilaterally or 'one-dimensionally' – which is one of the endless sources of misunderstanding in this debate. On the contrary, analyses that base themselves on the 'G-word' are everywhere giving rise to a *new emphasis on the local*.

That globalization does not only mean 'delocation' but also implies 'relocation' is already clear from the facts of economic calculation. In the literal sense of the word, no one can produce anything 'globally'. Firms which produce and market 'globally' must also develop *local* connections: that is, their production must be able to stand on local feet, and globally marketable symbols must be 'creamed' off local cultures (which therefore continue to remain lively and distinctive). 'Global', more mundanely translated, means 'in several places at once', or *translocal*.

It is no wonder, then, that this local–global nexus plays a central role in corporate calculation. Coca-Cola and Sony, for example, describe their strategy as 'global localization'. Their bosses and managers stress that the point of globalization is not to build factories everywhere in the world, but to become part of the respective culture. 'Localism' is what they call this strategy, which gains importance with the spread of globalization.

These inherent boundaries of linear cultural globalization, understood as uniform 'McDonaldization' of the world, may be visualized in the following extreme case. A single world culture pushed to its outer limits, where local cultures die out and everyone consumes, eats, sleeps, loves, dresses, argues and dreams in accordance with a single schema (however neatly divided by income group), would spell the end of the market, the end of profits. A world capitalism shaken by sales crises has a special need for local diversity and contrast, as a means of surviving competition through product and market innovation.

Nevertheless, delocation and relocation do not automatically mean renaissance of the local. To put it in terms familiar in Bavaria, we could say that the celebration of 'veal sausage', 'Löwenbräu beer' and 'lederhosen' does not offer salvation in the transition to the global era. For the revival of local colour suppresses the process of '*de*location'. And *re*location, which has already been through the infinitude of delocation, cannot be equated with a 'carry on as before' traditionalism and practised in a blinkered provincial spirit. The framework in which the meaning of the local has to establish itself has changed.

Delocation and relocation, taken together, certainly have a number of different consequences, but the most important is that local cultures can no longer be justified, shaped and renewed in seclusion from the rest of the world. In place of that knee-jerk defence of tradition by traditional means (which Anthony Giddens calls 'fundamentalism'), there is a compulsion to relocate detraditiona- lized traditions *within a global context* of exchange, dialogue and conflict.

In short, a non-traditionalist renaissance of the local occurs when local specificities are globally relocated and there conflictually renewed. To stay with the example of Bavaria, the 'veal sausage' may be redefined and represented as 'Hawaiian veal sausage'.

Glocalization: Roland Robertson

As we have seen, the workings of globalization usually lead to an *intensification of mutual dependence* beyond national boundaries. The model of separate worlds is thus, in a first stage, replaced with one of transnational interdependence. But Roland Robertson goes one crucial step further, by stressing how widely and deeply the 'awareness of the world as a single place' has become part of everyday reality.[21] For Robertson, then, globalization of the con- temporary world and *conscious* globalization *reflected in the mass media* are two sides of the same process. The generation of this cultural-symbolic reflexivity thus becomes the *key* question in the cultural sociology of globalization. The new human condition is a *conscious attention* to the globality and fragility of this human con- dition at the end of the twentieth century.

In this sense, globalization is not just a question of the 'objectiv- ity of growing interdependence'. What must be investigated, rather, is how the world horizon opens up in the cross-cultural production of meaning and cultural symbols. Cultural globaliza- tion thwarts the equation of national state with national society, by generating cross-cultural (and conflicting) modes of life and com- munication, attributions, responsibilities, self-images of groups and individuals and images they have of others. Elisabeth Beck- Gernsheim illustrates this by the example of cross-cultural mar- riages and families.

> Over and above all the various judgements, hopes and fears, one thing is certain: namely, that ethnic attributions – simply because of developments in society and the population structure – are becom- ing more and more complicated. For in the age of mobility, mass transport and economic linkage, there is a growing number of people who live and work with others beyond the radius of their

own original group; who for various reasons (whether hunger or persecution, education or occupation, travel or curiosity) leave their home country for a short or long period of time, perhaps for ever; who keep crossing borders, perhaps being born in one state and brought up in another, and marrying and having children in yet another. In the United States, this might already be becoming something 'quite normal': 'The number of bicultural partnerships is growing, and so it is no longer rare, for example, to be both white and Asian or Arab and Jewish' (R. C. Schneider). In Germany such mixed relationships are less common, but here too there is an unmistakable trend towards more 'colourful' family patterns. Take weddings, for example. In 1960 nearly everyone who married in the Federal Republic was German. Only in one case out of twenty-five – to quote the official statistics – were 'foreigners involved': that is, at least one of the partners had a foreign passport. By 1994, however, the man or woman or both were foreign citizens in one out of every seven marriage ceremonies. Or take the example of births. In 1960 children born in the Federal Republic nearly always issued from a 'purely German liaison' (in terms of citizenship); only 1.3 per cent had a foreign father or a foreign mother or both. By 1994 18.8 per cent of live births had a foreign father or mother or both – that is, nearly every fifth child issued from a German–foreign or wholly foreign liaison. This fast-growing group of 'transculturals' and their families poses the problem of social classification all the more sharply: where do they belong, to us, to the others, and to which others? What is involved here are variable, multifarious life-courses, which defy insertion into the established categories. This gives rise to complicated official procedures and discretionary issues, and obviously also to slips and mistakes in dealing with them.[22]

Some years ago, Jürgen Habermas was already speaking of a 'new obscurity', and Zygmunt Bauman speaks today of the 'end of clarity'. Local and global, Robertson argues, are not mutually exclusive.[23] On the contrary, the local must be understood as an *aspect* of the global. Globalization also means the drawing or coming together of local cultures, whose content has to be redefined in this 'clash of localities'. Robertson proposes replacing the concept of cultural globalization with that of '*glocalization*' – through a combination of the words 'global' and 'local'.

This new amalgam, 'glocalization', serves to underline the main claim of cultural theory: namely, that it is *absurd* to think we can understand the contemporary world, with all its breakdowns and new departures, without grasping what is expressed in the keywords 'politics of culture, cultural capital, cultural difference, cultural homogeneity, ethnicity, race and gender'.[24]

It is no exaggeration to say that this is precisely the dividing-line between old 'world-system' approaches and the new, culturally attuned 'sociology of globalization'.

The carefully polished axiom which separates the wheat from the chaff is as follows. 'Global culture' cannot be understood as a static phenomenon, but only as a *contingent* and *dialectical process* (which is *not* economistically reducible to some one-sided logic of capital), in accordance with a model of 'glocalization' in which contradictory elements are conceived and deciphered *in their unity*. It is in this sense that one may speak of paradoxes of 'glocal' cultures.

This axiom has an important methodological-pragmatic application. Globalization – which seems to be the super-dimension, appearing at the end from outside and overshadowing everything else – can be grasped in the small and concrete, in the spatially particular, in one's own life, in cultural symbols that all bear the signature of the 'glocal'.

This may also be explained by saying that the sociology of globalization becomes *empirically possible* and necessary only as a 'glocal' cultural investigation of industry, inequality, technology and politics.

But what is meant by this word 'dialectical' which, having been dismissed by all clear-headed thinkers, now suddenly returns to the fore in cultural theory? What does globalization signify when conceptualized and investigated as a 'flow'?[25]

Universalism and particularism   The growing worldwide uniformity of institutions, symbols and behaviour (McDonald's, blue jeans, democracy, information technology, banks, human rights, etc.) is not contradicted by the new emphasis on, the new discovery and defence of, local cultures and identities (Islamicization, renationalization, German pop and North African rai, Afro-Caribbean street carnival in London or Hawaiian veal sausage). Indeed, to take the example of human rights, they are presented in nearly every culture as universal rights, but at the same time they are interpreted and represented in often quite different ways according to the context.

Connection and fragmentation   Globalization generates (compels) bonding. It is necessary to stress this, since the discussion of globalization deprecates it and virtually equates it with fragmentation. There emerge transnational or transcontinental 'communities' (this word needs to be redefined) which divide what has often long been seen as an indissoluble unit: they create the basis for geographical and social coexistence and cooperation, but also for a new form of social bonding. This new logic of living and working together in separate places is practised both in transnational corporations (whose offices may be moved to Singapore while production is distributed all over Europe) and in transnational 'communities' (Mexican Americans, American Mexicans), 'families', 'ethnic subcultures' (an imagined Africa), and so on.

For the same reason, however, it is true that globalization *fragments*: not only does it undermine the control of individual states over information and taxes, and therefore their authority in general; it may also lead to the destruction of local communities. Under the conditions of global culture, it is quite possible in extreme cases that direct relations between neighbouring countries will be abandoned, while transnational 'neighbourhoods' flourish. It is possible, not by any means necessary.

Centralization and decentralization   Many people see globalization quite one-sidedly as a process of concentration and centralization – in the dimensions of capital, power, information, knowledge, wealth, decision-making, etc. – and the reasons they give are often good. But this overlooks the fact that the same dynamic also generates *de*centralization. Local – or, to be more precise, translocal – communities acquire influence by shaping their social spaces, but they also do this in their respective local (that is, national) contexts.

National states may cut themselves off from the outside world. But they may just as well adopt an active orientation towards it, relocating and redefining their politics and identity in the global context of mutual relationships, dialogue and conflict. The same is true of actors at all levels, including intermediate ones, of social existence – from trade unions through churches or consumer associations right down to individuals.

Conflict and balance   It is not difficult to imagine the glocal as a world disintegrating into conflicts. In a sense, even the vision of a 'war of cultures' – for all its peculiarly horrific content – remains stuck in the children's shoes of the national state. For glocalization also means that conflict appears in the place of local ties of communality, and that 'disflict' appears in the place of conflict (which always assumes at least a minimum of integration). One has only to think of a division of the world triggered by *exclusion* of those 'without purchasing power' – perhaps the future majority of mankind – and hence a *Brazilianization* of the world.[26]

But this eerie and far from groundless vision inevitably raises the question of why it *one-sidedly* emphasizes only this aspect of the future. For while these gloomy prospects must not be covered up or glossed over, it seems to have gone unnoticed that glocalization also produces new kinds of 'communality'. These range from Mickey Mouse and Coca-Cola through the symbolism of poisoned dying creatures (images of oil-soaked seagulls and baby seals) to the first signs of a world public sphere which, funnily enough, manifested themselves in the transnational Shell boycott.

A little while back, Fukuyama was still announcing the 'end of history'. Howard Perlmutter was right to counter this by talking of the beginnings of a history of *global* civilization,[27] in which globalization becomes *reflexive* and thus gains a new historical quality that justifies the term 'world society'. For this presupposes *experiences of a common destiny*, which is expressed in the quite incredible proximity of the faraway within a world without frontiers.

Excursus: two modes of distinction   In this connection (and also to clarify the concept of 'dialectics'), I would propose to distinguish in general between *exclusive* and *inclusive* modes of distinction. Exclusive distinctions follow the logic of Either-Or. They delineate the world as a coordination and subordination of separate worlds, in which identities and memberships are mutually exclusive. Anything falling in between [*jeder Zwischen-Fall*] is a passing incident [*Zwischenfall*]. It may confuse and scandalize, forcing repression or activities to restore order.

Inclusive distinctions, on the other hand, draw a quite different picture of 'order'. To fall between the categories is here not an exception but the rule. If this appears scandalous, it is only because the motley image of inclusive distinctions challenges the 'naturalness' of models of exclusive classification.

One advantage of inclusive distinctions is, of course, that they facilitate a different, more mobile and, if you like, cooperative concept of 'borders'. Here borders arise not through exclusion but through particularly solid forms of 'double inclusion'. Someone, for example, is part of a large number of circles and is circumscribed *by that*. (Sociologically speaking, it is quite obvious that, although this is not the only way in which borders can be conceived and lived, it may be an important way in the future.) In the framework of inclusive distinctions, therefore, borders are conceived and strengthened as mobile patterns that facilitate over-lapping loyalties.

In the paradigm of exclusive distinction, globalization is no more than a limiting case that blows everything apart. Here, globalization must appear as the peak of a development that cancels all distinctions and establishes the undifferentiatable in their place. The methodological consequence is that a grand totality can perhaps suddenly be viewed again. But it is clear that this view will suffer from eye strain, and may even shatter as a result.

For the paradigm of inclusive distinction, by contrast, there is above all a pragmatic *research argument*: namely, that *it alone makes possible the sociological investigation of globality*. The new hybrid of world and ego that appears here has given sociology a new foundation, for without sociology it can be neither theoretically-empirically conceived and studied nor politically handled. The assumption of inclusive distinctions thus acquires the status of an *empirical working hypothesis*, one which, in the adventures of current research, must be driven out into the unknown world society in which we live. What is logically subordinate in Either-Or thinking – the 'inclusive' forms of life, biography, conflict, rule, inequality and state typical of world society – must at least be spelt out and thoroughly investigated. But inclusive distinctions, too, can and must be *clearly* drawn.[28] To adapt something that Gottfried Benn once said, woolly thinking and an inability to make distinctions do not add up to a theory of reflexive modernization.

The power of imagining possible lives: Arjun Appadurai

Robertson's analysis of 'glocal' cultures has been taken further by Arjun Appadurai, who affirms and theorizes the *relative autonomy* and distinctive logic of a glocal culture and economy. In this connection Appadurai speaks of *ethnoscapes* or 'landscapes of people' such as tourists, immigrants, refugees, exiles, *Gastarbeiter* and other groups on the move, which mark the unsettled, friable world in which we live. They and their physical restlessness set up major impulses toward a change in politics within and between nations; they are one aspect of the face of global culture. Alongside ethnoscapes, Appadurai also identifies and describes:

- *Technoscapes*: cross-border movements of new and old technologies, based on both machines and computers.

- *Financescapes*: huge sums of money moving between countries with incredible speed, by means of currency markets, national stock exchanges and speculative enterprises.
- *Mediascapes*: the distribution of opportunities for the production and dissemination of electronic images.
- *Ideoscapes*: the interlinking of images, often in connection with state or opposition ideologies and ideas which have their roots in the Enlightenment.[29]

As Appadurai shows, these flows of images and landscapes also call into question the traditional distinction between centre and periphery. They are cornerstones of *'imagined worlds'* that are provided with different meanings as they are exchanged and experienced by people and groups around the globe.

'On a political map,' writes K. Ohmae,

> the boundaries between countries are as clear as ever. [...But] of all the forces eating them away, perhaps the most persistent is the flow of information – information that governments previously monopolized. [...] Their monopoly of knowledge about things happening around the world enabled them to fool, mislead, or control the people. [...] Today [...] people everywhere are more and more able to get the information they want directly from all corners of the world.

The emerging global cultures, adds A. D. Smith, are 'tied to no place or period'. They are 'context-less, a true mélange of disparate components drawn from everywhere and nowhere, borne upon the modern (postmodern) chariots of global communications systems'.[30]

What does this mean? Imagination gains a special kind of power in people's everyday lives, answers Appadurai.[31] More people in more parts of the world dream of and consider a greater range of 'possible' lives than they have ever done before. A central source of this are the mass media, which offer a wide and constantly changing supply of such 'possible lives'. In this way, an imaginary closeness to symbolic media figures is also created. The spectacles through which people perceive and evaluate their lives, hopes, setbacks and present situations are made up of the prisms of possible lives which 'tele-vision' constantly presents and celebrates.

Even people fixed to the most hopeless and brutal situations in life – child labourers, for example, or those who live by rummaging through city refuse – are nevertheless open to the sinister play of the imagination fabricated by the culture industry. Impoverishment is refracted, perhaps even duplicated, in the glittering, enticing commodity forms of possible life that lurid advertising everywhere proclaims.

This new power of global imagination industries means that local lifestyles are diluted and stirred around with 'models' whose social and spatial origins lie somewhere altogether different. People's own lives and possible lives thus enter at least into ironical conflict with each other. For, as we have seen, even impoverishment is placed under the market power of imaginary lives, remaining locked into the global circulation of images and models which (actively and passively) keeps the cultural economy going.

Global wealth, local poverty: Zygmunt Bauman

Let us sum up. British and American observers of the global scenery who received a training in cultural theory have taken leave of what might be called the 'McDonaldization of the world' thesis. It is agreed that globalization does *not* necessarily bring about cultural uniformity, and that the mass production of cultural symbols and information does *not* lead to the emergence of anything like a 'global culture'. Rather, the developing glocal scenery should be seen as a blatantly ambivalent 'imagining of possible lives' that permits a multiplicity of combinations. Indeed, for the purposes of one's life and group identities, sharply varying and motley collections are put together out of that range of possibilities.

For Zygmunt Bauman, different kinds of identity are woven with the global thread of cultural symbols. The local self-differentiation industry is becoming one of the (globally determined) hallmarks of the late twentieth century. The global consumer goods and information markets make a selection of what is to be absorbed unavoidable – but the type and mode of the choice are decided locally or communally, so as to provide new symbolic characteristics for the reawakened, reinvented or so far merely postulated identities. Bauman concludes that the community, rediscovered by a new breed of Romantic admirers who see it threatened by dark forces of deracination and depersonalization, is not the antidote to globalization but one of its inevitable global consequences – product and precondition at one and the same time.

In order to complete this stage in the argument concerning the distinctive logic involved in a dimension of globalization, let us now look at some crucial and disturbing consequences of global inequalities. According to Bauman, the global–local nexus does not simply permit or enforce new analytical-empirical modes of considering translocal cultures and lifeworlds; it actually splits the approaching world society. Globalization and localization are thus not only two moments or aspects of the same thing. They are at once driving forces and expressions of a new *polarization and stratification of the world population into globalized rich and localized poor*.

For Bauman, then, globalization and localization may be two sides of the same coin, but the two sections of the world's population live on different sides and see only one of the sides – rather as people on earth see only one side of the moon. Some have the planet as their residence, while others are chained to the spot. 'Glocalization' is first and foremost a 'redistribution of privileges and deprivations, of wealth and poverty, of resources and impotence, of power and powerlessness, of freedom and constraint'.

Glocalization is

> the process of a *world-wide restratification*, in the course of which a new socio-cultural hierarchy, on a world-wide scale, is put together. The quasi-sovereignties, territorial divisions and segregations of identities which the globalization of markets and information promotes and renders 'a must', do not reflect diversity of equal partners. What is a free choice for some descends as cruel fate upon others. And since those 'others' tend to grow unstoppably in numbers and sink ever deeper into despair born of a prospectless existence, one will be well advised to speak of *'glocalization'* [...] and to define it mostly as the process of the concentration of capital, finance and all other resources of choice and effective action, but also – perhaps above all – of the *concentration of freedom* to move and to act.

According to what Bauman calls the 'folkloristic beliefs of the new generation of enlightened classes',

> freedom (of trade and capital mobility, first and foremost) is the hothouse in which wealth would grow faster than ever before; and once the wealth is multiplied, there will be more of it for everybody. The poor of the world – whether old or new, hereditary or computer-made – would hardly recognize their plight in this folkloristic fiction. [...] The old rich needed the poor to make and keep them

rich. That dependency at all times mitigated the conflict of interest and prompted some effort, however tenuous, to care. The new rich do not need the poor any more. At long last the bliss of ultimate freedom is nigh.

As a matter of fact, the worlds sedimented on the two poles, at the top and at the bottom of the emergent hierarchy of mobility, differ sharply; they also become increasingly incommunicado to each other. For the first world, the world of the globally mobile, the space has lost its constraining quality and is easily traversed in both its 'real' and 'virtual' renditions. For the second world, the world of the 'locally tied', of those barred from moving and thus bound to bear passively whatever change may be visited on the locality they are tied to, the real space is fast closing up. This is a kind of deprivation which is made yet more painful by the obtrusive media display of the space conquest and of the *'virtual* access-ibility' of distances that stay stubbornly unreachable in non-virtual reality.

The shrinking of space abolishes the flow of time. The inhabitants of the first world live in a perpetual present, going through a succession of episodes hygienically insulated from their past as well as their future. These people are constantly busy and perpe-tually 'short of time', since each moment of time is non-extensive – an experience identical with that of time 'full to the brim'. People marooned in the opposite world are crushed under the burden of abundant, redundant and useless time they have nothing to fill with. In their time 'nothing ever happens'. They do not 'con-trol' time – but neither are they controlled by it, unlike their clocking-in, clocking-out ancestors, subject to the faceless rhythm of factory time. They can only kill time, as they are slowly killed by it.

Residents of the first world live in *time*; space does not matter for them, since spanning every distance is instantaneous. It is this experience which Jean Baudrillard encapsulated in his image of 'hyperreality', where the virtual and the real are no longer separ-able, since both share or miss in the same measure that 'objectivity', 'externality' and 'punishing power' which Émile Durkheim listed as the symptoms of all reality. Residents of the second world, on the contrary, live in *space*: heavy, resilient, untouchable, which ties down time and keeps it beyond the residents' control. Their time is void; in their time, 'nothing ever happens'. Only the virtual, TV time has a structure, a 'timetable' – the rest of time is monotonously ticking away; it comes and goes, making no demands and appar-ently leaving no trace. Its sediments appear all of a sudden, unan-nounced and uninvited, immaterial and light-weight, ephemeral, with nothing to fill it with sense and so give it gravity, time has no power over that all-too-real space to which the residents of the second world are confined.

As far as the rich 'inhabitants of the first world' are concerned, the poor or the vagabonds whom they glimpse on their travels

> are not really able to afford the kind of sophisticated choices in which the consumers are expected to excel. [...] This fault makes their position in society precarious. They are useless, in the sole sense of 'use' one can think of in a society of consumers or society of tourists. And because they are useless, they are also unwanted.[32]

What is new in the global age is this loss of the nexus between poverty and wealth. For globalization splits the world's population into the globalized rich, who overcome space and never have enough time, and the localized poor, who are chained to the spot and can only 'kill' time.

Between these winners and losers of globalization, Bauman argues, there will in future be *no* unity and *no* ties of dependence. The most important result is that the master–slave dialectic breaks down. Or rather, the bond that made some kind of solidarity not only necessary but possible loosens and dissolves. The relationship of dependence, or at least sympathy, which has lain at the basis of all previous historical forms of inequality, falls away in the new Nowhere of world society. Consequently, even the term 'glocalization' is a euphemism. It hides the fact that conditions are being generated *beyond* unity and dependence for which we have no name and know no answer.

Capitalism without work

Two points qualify Bauman's important argument that globalization is leading to a polarization of rich and poor on a world scale. In a way, he may be said to overlook himself. For at least in *his* perspective as observer, he *binds together* what he depicts as irrevocably disintegrated in trans-state world society: namely, the framework, the *minima moralia*, which make the poor appear as *our* poor, and the rich as *our* rich.

But the formation of a 'cosmopolitan solidarity' (Habermas) cannot be ruled out, even if it would have a weaker bonding power than the citizenship solidarity which grew up in Europe in the course of one to two centuries. And world societies do not only undermine nationally structured and controlled communities; they also create a new closeness between seemingly separate worlds – not only 'out there' but also here and now, in people's own ordinary lives. In a crucial sense (to take up Appadurai, for example), it is even questionable whether in the second modernity the cultural production of 'possible lives' – which literally includes or 'locks in' the richest and poorest alike – allows any groups at all to be excluded.[33]

The first world is contained in the third and fourth worlds, just as the third and fourth are contained in the first. Neither centre nor periphery can be identified with separate continents; here *and* there, both conflict with each other in a variety of hybrid relationships. This new impossibility of excluding the poor can be seen in Rio, for example, where the homeless 'occupy' luxury streets at nightfall.

Bauman does not adequately explain why globalization destroys even a modicum of community between rich and poor. Therefore we will take this question up here and ask: is work disappearing from the work society?[34]

'The future of work looks like this at our company', said the boss of BMW. And then he drew a line beginning in 1970 and falling to zero by the year 2000.

> Of course that's an exaggeration, and we can't put it like that in public. But productivity is increasing to such an extent that we can produce more and more cars with less and less work. Just to keep the employment level stable, we would have to expand our markets enormously. Only if we sell BMWs in every corner of the world is there any chance at all of keeping existing jobs.

Capitalism is doing away with work. Unemployment is no longer a marginal fate: it affects everyone potentially, as well as the democratic way of life.[35] But in abrogating responsibility for employment and democracy, global capitalism undermines its own legitimacy. Before a new Marx shakes up the West, some long-overdue ideas and models for a different social contract will need to be taken up again. The future of democracy beyond the work society must be given a new foundation.

In Britain, for example, the country so much praised for its jobs record, only a third of people capable of gainful employment are fully employed in the classical sense of the term, against more than 60 per cent still in Germany. Twenty years ago, the figure in both countries was above 80 per cent. What is presented as a rescue remedy – the flexibilization of paid employment – has concealed and displaced, not cured, the disease of unemployment. Indeed everything is now rising: the numbers of unemployed and the grey area of part-time work, the insecurity of employment conditions, and the hidden reserves of labour. In other words, the quantity of paid labour is rapidly shrinking. We are approaching a capitalism without work, in all the post-industrial countries of the world.

Three myths screen public debate from the reality of the situation: first, everything is much too complicated anyway (the unfathomability myth); second, the coming upturn in the service sector will save the work society (the services myth); and third, we have only to drive down wage-costs and the problem of unemployment will vanish (the costs myth).

That everything is connected (however weakly) to everything else, and is to that extent unfathomable, certainly applies to the development of the labour market under conditions of globalization. But this does not preclude statements about secular trends, such as the internationally comparable longitudinal sections commissioned or compiled by the German Commission for Issues of the Future.[36] According to its recent report, the value of the labour factor was constantly increasing over a number of generations, until a break occurred in the middle of the seventies. Since then, the amount of paid employment has everywhere been declining – either directly in the form of unemployment (as in Germany) or indirectly through the exponential growth of 'hybrid forms of employment' (as in the United States or Britain). Demand for labour has been decreasing, while the supply of labour has been increasing (also as a result of globalization). The two indicators of a decline in gainful employment – joblessness and unregulated labour – have set the alarm bells ringing.

For a long time now it has been a question not of redistributing work but of *redistributing unemployment* – including in the new hybrids of employment and unemployment (short-term contracts, 'junk jobs', part-time work, etc.), which are officially counted in the category of 'full employment'. This is true especially in the employment paradises of the USA and Britain, where a majority have for some time been living in the grey area between work and non-work, often having to make do with starvation wages.

Yet there are many who close their eyes to the fact that the soup of the work society is getting thinner with every fresh crisis, and that ever larger sections of the population have only in-secure 'little jobs' which can hardly be said to provide a stable existence.   .

Politicians, institutions and indeed we ourselves think in the fictitious terms of a world of full employment. Even building socie-ties and insurance companies conclude their deals on the assump-tion that 'employed' people will continue to have a stable income. The rapidly spreading category of the Neither-Nor – neither unem-ployed nor income-secure – does not fit into that stereotype.

Mothers give up their job when they have children. But the three-phase model in terms of which they operate is no longer applicable. The third phase – a return to their previous work after the children have left home – is based upon the illusion of full employment. We complain about 'mass unemployment', but at the same time we assume that a full-time job is an adult's natural state right up to the age of retirement. In this emphatic sense, the GDR too was a work society. Now it is necessary to dwell on the extensive unemployment in the new federal *Länder* of Eastern Germany.

Many think, hope and pray that the service society can save us from the evil dragon of unemployment. This is the *services myth*. The rival calculations still have to be put to the test. It is certainly true that new jobs will come into being. But first, on the contrary, the traditionally secure core of employment in the service sector will be sacrificed to a wave of automation that is only just begin-ning. For example, telebanking will lead to the closure of high-street banks; telecommunications will shed some 60,000 jobs through a process of consolidation; and whole occupational cate-gories, such as typists, may simply disappear.

Even if new jobs do emerge, in this computer age they can easily be transferred anywhere in the world. Many firms – American Express being the most recent example – are switching whole sections of their administration to low-wage countries (in this case, southern India).

Contrary to the prophets of the information society, who predict an abundance of highly paid jobs even for people with only basic education, the sobering truth is that numerous jobs even in data-processing will be poorly paid routine activities. The foot-soldiers of the information economy – according to Clinton's former labour minister, the economist Robert Reich – are hordes of data-proces-sors sitting at back-room computer terminals linked to worldwide databases.

The key illusion in current debate, however, is the *costs myth*. More and more people are infected with the (often very militant) conviction that only a radical lowering of labour costs will lead us out of the vale of unemployment. Here the 'American way' is held up as our beacon, yet it is clearly one that involves deep division. According to OECD statistics published in April 1996, jobs for the highly skilled (which are still secure and well paid) have been appearing just as rarely or as often in the United States as they have in high-wage Germany – by an extra 2.6 per cent a year. The real difference between the two countries is in the growth of low-paid unskilled jobs. What characterizes the 'American miracle' is the rise of *minor services*, but it must be emphasized that this presupposes an open immigration policy. In future, admittedly, an unemployed graduate in Munich may find himself compelled to pick asparagus in the villages of Lower Bavaria. Both the asparagus and the asparagus-growers will have cause to regret this, however, because he will have neither the skills nor the motivation that a Polish agricultural labourer would bring to what he would see as a generally better job.

The negative aspects of the American jobs miracle are the following. From 1979 to 1989, workers' incomes on the bottom tenth of the jobs ladder fell by a further 16 per cent. Even in middle grades real incomes fell by 2 per cent, and only at the top did they actually rise – by 5 per cent. This downward trend may, it is true, have been halted for the 'working poor' in the period between 1989 and 1997 – after all, those who already receive the rock-bottom wage for their work can hardly take another cut. For the majority of middle-grade American workers, however, average incomes have fallen since 1989 by a further 5 per cent. For the first time, we are dealing with an upturn in the economy in which 'full employment' is *accompanied* by declining real incomes in the middle levels of society.[37] 'Great,' one said, 'Bill Clinton has created millions of new jobs.' – 'Yes,' answered another, 'I've got three of them and I can't keep my family.' In Germany, by contrast, it is still (!) thought a problem that people who work all day for, say, 7 marks an hour should sleep at night in cardboard boxes.

Furthermore, even a comparison of labour productivity takes the gloss off the American 'solution'. Over the past twenty years, average productivity in the United States has risen by no more than 25 per cent, as opposed to 100 per cent in Germany. 'Just how do the Germans manage that?' an American colleague asked me recently. 'They work less and produce more.'

This is precisely where the new law of productivity of global capitalism makes itself apparent in the information age. A smaller and smaller number of well-educated, globally interchangeable people can produce more and more goods and services. Economic growth, then, no longer triggers a reduction in unemployment but, on the contrary, presupposes a reduction in the number of jobs – what has been called 'jobless growth'.

Let there be no mistake. An owner-capitalism which aims only to increase profits, taking no account of employees, the welfare state and democracy, undermines its own legitimacy. While globally active enterprises secure higher profit margins, they withdraw both jobs and fiscal revenue from more expensive countries and burden others with the costs of unemployment and developed civilization. Two chronic seats of poverty – the public purse and the private purse of those still in employment – are alone supposed to finance what the rich also enjoy by way of the 'luxuries' of the second modernity: high-quality schools and universities, a smoothly functioning transport system, protection of the country-side, safe streets, all the colour and variety of urban life.

If global capitalism in the highly developed countries of the West dissolves the core values of the work society, a historical link between capitalism, welfare state and democracy will break apart. Democracy in Europe and North America came into the world as 'labour democracy', in the sense that it rested upon participation in gainful employment. Citizens had to earn their money in one way or another, in order to breathe life into political rights and freedoms. Paid labour has always underpinned not only private but also political existence. What is at issue today, then, is not 'only' the millions of unemployed, nor only the future of the welfare state, the struggle against poverty, or the possibility of greater social justice. Everything we have is at stake. Political free-dom and democracy in Europe are at stake.

The Western association of capitalism with basic political, social and economic rights is not some 'social favour' to be dispensed with when money gets tight. Rather, socially buffered capitalism was a gain that answered the experience of fascism and the chal-lenge of communism. As an applied form of Enlightenment, it rests upon the realization that only people who have a home and a secure job, and therefore a material future, are or can become citizens for whom democracy is a living reality of their own mak-ing. The simple truth is that without material security there is no political freedom and no democracy, only a threat to everyone from new and old totalitarian regimes and ideologies.

Thus, it is not the fact that capitalism produces more and more with less and less labour, but the fact that it blocks any initiative towards a new social contract, which is robbing it of legitimacy. Anyone today who thinks about unemployment should not remain a prisoner of old concepts by arguing over the 'second labour market', the 'part-time offensive', the so-called 'benefits not covered by insurance' or the payment of wages in case of sickness. What should be asked instead is how democracy will be possible without the securities of the work society. What appears as ending and decay must be interpreted in a different light, at a time when new ideas and models are being laid for the state, economy and society of the twenty-first century.[38]

2

Transnational Civil Society: How a Cosmopolitan Vision is Emerging

'Methodological nationalism' and its refutation: a provisional appraisal

Why and in what sense does globalization force us to distinguish between a first and a second age of modernity? The understanding of society that characterized the first modernity has been aptly described by A. D. Smith as 'methodological nationalism': society and state were conceived, organized and experienced as coextensive.

This presupposed the political definition and control of space by the state. The territorial state became the 'container' of society. Or, to put it in another way, the state's claim to exercise power and control was the foundation of society. This primacy of the national can and should be analysed in respect of the various basic rights, the education system, social policy, the party landscape, taxes, language, history, literature, transport, infrastructure, passport and frontier controls, and so on.

National societies also generate and preserve in this way the quasi-essentialist identities of everyday life, whose self-evidence seems to derive from such tautological formulations as: Germans live in Germany, Japanese in Japan, Africans in Africa. That there are 'black Jews' or 'Greek Germans' – to take just a couple of trivial instances in the quite normal confusion of world society – is seen within this horizon as a limiting case or exception, and thus as a threat.[1]

This architecture of thinking, acting and living within state-cum-social spaces and identities *collapses* in the course of economic, political, ecological, cultural and biographical globalization. World society means the emergence of new power opportunities and new social spaces for action, living and perception, which break up and muddle the nation-state orthodoxy of politics and society.

(1)   This is most conspicuous where transnational corporations are given the opportunity to spread jobs and taxes around on the world chessboard in such a way that, as before, they maximize their profits whilst (not necessarily intentionally) depriving the developed social-welfare states of active opportunities to mould their society. This example is typical in that all the features of the new power and conflict structure between national states and world-society players can be detected in it. What is novel and decisive is not that these transnational corporations are growing in number and diversity, but that, in the course of globalization, they are placed in a position *to play off national states against one another*.

Looked at from outside, everything has remained as it was. Companies produce, rationalize, hire and fire, pay taxes, and so on. The crucial point, however, is that they no longer do this under rules of the game defined by national states, but continue to play the old game while nullifying and redefining those rules. It thus only *appears* to be a question of the old game of labour and capital, state and unions. For while one player continues to play the game within the framework of the national state, the other is already playing within the framework of world society.

In the relationship between the first and the second modernity, we are therefore no longer dealing with a rule-governed but with a *rule-changing* politics, or, as I have put it elsewhere, with a *politics of politics* or a *metapolitics*.[2]

This is characterized by the fact that the new power game between national and transnational players is acted out in the familiar rules and colours of the distribution struggle of industrial society. It is as if employees, unions and government were still playing draughts, while the transnational corporations had moved on to chess. What looks like a draughtsman may thus become a knight in the hands of a corporation, which may then suddenly deliver checkmate to a thunderstruck national king.

(2)   As Appadurai has shown most clearly, the equation of state, society and identity is also cancelled by the symbolic world of global culture industries. The imagining of possible lives can no

longer be conceived as national or ethnic or as corresponding to the polarity of rich and poor; it can only be understood as taking place within world society. What people dream, how they would like to be, their everyday utopias of happiness – these are no longer tied to a particular geographical area and its cultural identities. Even urban rummagers live in and from the garbage of world society, and remain linked into the symbolic circuits of global culture industries.

In this sense, the collapse of the Eastern bloc was also manifestly a result of cultural globalization. The 'iron curtain' and the military counter-espionage service dissolved into nothingness in the television age. Television advertising, for example, which is often scorned by cultural criticism in the West, changed in an environment of shortage and regimentation into a fused promise of consumption and political freedom.

(3) This becomes understandable only when one clearly distinguishes two concepts of culture that are usually confused.

> The first concept of culture (culture 1) views culture as essentially territorial; it assumes that culture stems from a learning-process that is, in the main, localized. This is culture in the sense of *a culture*, that is, the culture of a society or social group. A notion that goes back to nineteenth-century romanticism and that has been elaborated in twentieth-century anthropology, in particular cultural relativism – with the notion of cultures as a whole, a Gestalt, configuration. [...] A wider understanding of culture (culture 2) views culture as a general human 'software'. This notion has been implicit in theories of evolution and diffusion, in which culture is viewed as, in the main, a *translocal* learning process.

Culture 2 necessarily means cultures *in the plural*. These are conceived as a non-integrated, non-separated multiplicity without unity, in the sense of what I have referred to as inclusive distinctions.

> These understandings are not incompatible: culture 2 finds expression in culture 1, cultures are the vehicle of culture. But they do reflect different emphases in relation to historical processes of culture formation. [...] Culture 2 or translocal culture is not without place (there is no culture without place), but it involves an *outward-looking* sense of place, whereas culture 1 is based on an *inward-looking* sense of place. Culture 2 involves what Doreen Massey

calls 'a global sense of place': 'the specificity of place which derives from the fact that each place is the focus of a distinct *mixture* of wider and more local social relations'.

The general terminology of cultural pluralism, multicultural society, intercultural relations, etc. does not clarify whether it refers to culture 1 or culture 2. Thus, relations among cultures can be viewed in a static fashion (in which cultures retain their separateness in interaction) or a fluid fashion (in which cultures interpenetrate).[3]

In other words, the distinction between culture 1 and culture 2 may be seen as a further stone in the mosaic that distinguishes the first and second modernities.

(4) Bauman refers to a central problem arising out of 'glocalization': namely, that rich and poor no longer sit at the same (distributive) table of the national state. Why should winners from globalization, if they are ever troubled at all by pangs of conscience, distribute their horn of plenty precisely in the rich countries of Europe? Why not promote democratic self-help organizations in Africa and South America? Just like poverty or profits, *compassion is also becoming global*. Whereas the *citoyen* is still trapped in the framework of the national state, the *bourgeois* acts in a cosmopolitan manner – which means that when his democratic heart throbs, his action no longer has to obey the imperatives of national loyalty.

(5) The ambiguity of globalizations in the plural includes the fact that, in a kind of build-up effect, *supranational and subnational regionalisms* come into being. A good example of this is the European Union. Having arisen as a response to world-market competition from the United States and Japan, the developing European institutional structure mainly appeared as an internal market. The introduction of the euro, however, means the emergence not only of a common currency area but also of political-administrative pressure to solve the electoral and other resulting problems. In this way, the still largely separate nations and cultures – France, Germany, Spain, etc. – are being broken up from within and forced to join themselves to one another. What has previously lain hidden is thus becoming visible: namely, that there are not one but *many Europes* – a Europe of nations, a Europe of regions, a Europe of civilizations, a Europe of Christianities, and so on.

The dialectics of [European] unification mean, for instance, that constituencies in Northern Ireland can appeal to the European Court of Human Rights in Strasbourg on decisions of the British courts, or that Catalonia can outflank Madrid and Brittany outmanoeuvre Paris by appealing to Brussels or by establishing links with other regions (for example, between Catalonia and the Ruhr area). Again there is an ongoing flow or cascade of globalization – regionalism – sub-regionalism. Or [as R. W. Cox puts it], 'Globalization encourages macro-regionalism, which, in turn, encourages micro-regionalism. Micro-regionalism in poor areas will be a means not only of affirming cultural identities but of claiming pay-offs at the macro-regional level for maintaining political stability and economic good behaviour. The issues of redistribution are thereby raised from the sovereign state level to the macro-regional level, while the manner in which redistributed wealth is used becomes decentralized to the micro-regional level.' What globalization means in structural terms, then, is *the increase in the available modes of organization*: transnational, international, macro-regional, national, micro-regional, municipal, local. This ladder of administrative levels is being crisscrossed by *functional networks* of corporations, international organizations and non-governmental organizations, as well as by professionals and computer users.[4]

In what follows, the first (national) modernity and its basic assumptions will be contrasted with the concept (the features, questions and assumptions) of *global civil society*. (a) What is the meaning of *globalization from below*? How do cosmopolitan initiatives become possible? (b) What are the action resources and power opportunities of a *transnational civil society*? (c) What does *globalization of biographies* mean? How is a *cosmopolitan vision* emerging? (d) What do cross-cultural tolerance and criticism mean, and what makes them possible?

Symbolically staged mass boycotts: cosmopolitan initiatives and global subpolitics

In the summer of 1995 the modern hero for the cause, Greenpeace, succeeded in getting the oil multinational Shell to dispose of an old drilling platform on land, instead of in the North Atlantic. Then this multinational action organization, in order to prevent France's resumption of atomic bomb testing, publicly accused President Chirac of deliberately breaking the rules (although this time it did not succeed in its aim). It began to seem to many that, if an unauthorized player such as Greenpeace conducted its own global domestic policy without regard for national sovereignty and diplomatic norms, some of the most basic principles of foreign policy were going by the board. Tomorrow it might be the Moonies, and then some private organization, which would seek to bestow its favours upon the common weal.

We should be clear, however, that the oil company was brought to its knees not by Greenpeace but by a mass citizens' boycott, organized by means of a worldwide television indictment. The truth is that Greenpeace, instead of shaking the political system, made visible the vacuum of power and legitimacy at the heart of that system, which in many respects parallels what happened in the GDR. Later it became clear that Greenpeace had been playing with false cards, greatly exaggerating the extent of the feared damage to the North Sea. This undermined for some time the credibility of the 'knight in shining armour', but the political scenario remained in place for future possible action.

This coalition pattern of global subpolitics and direct politics is seen over and over again. Alliances appear between those who are not 'really' capable of allying with each other. Thus the former German Chancellor Helmut Kohl supported the Greenpeace action against the then British prime minister, John Major. Political elements were suddenly uncovered or deployed in everyday actions such as filling up at a petrol station. Car drivers joined forces against the oil industry. (This meant as much, after all, as drug addicts practising rebellion against their dealer.) In the end, the state power made a coalition with the illegitimate action and its organizers. The state thus sanctioned the deliberate, extra-parliamentary breach involved in direct-action politics, which had precisely tried to escape the narrow framework of indirect, official bodies and regulations through a kind of 'self-administered ecological justice'. The anti-Shell alliance could be said to have completed a scene change between the politics of the first and the second modernity: national governments sat on the spectator benches, while unauthorized actors of the second modernity decided what would be done on stage.

The political novelty, then, was not that David defeated Goliath, but that David *plus* Goliath, acting globally, banded together first against a world corporation and then against a national government and its policy. The novelty was the round-the-globe alliance between extra-parliamentary and parliamentary forces, citizens and governments, for a cause that was in a higher sense legitimate: the saving of the earth's environment.

Of course, the anti-Shell alliance was morally dubious; to be quite frank, it was based on hypocrisy. Helmut Kohl, for instance, by striking a symbolic attitude that cost him nothing, was able to gloss over the fact that his policy acceptance of high speeds on German motorways was polluting the air in Europe.

Just beneath the surface, German Green nationalism and attitudes of superiority were doubtless struggling to gain a voice. Many Germans would like to have a kind of Green Greater Switzerland; they dream of a Germany that is the world's ecological conscience. But the lessons of politics are different from those of morality. Precisely in this alliance of mutually exclusive persuasions – from Chancellor Kohl to Greenpeace activists, from Porsche fetishists to incendiaries – we can see the new quality of the political.

The activity of global corporations and national governments has come under pressure from world public opinion. Individual and collective participation in nexuses of global action is here the remarkable and decisive factor. *Citizens are discovering that the act of purchase can always and everywhere be a direct ballot-paper*. The boycott can thus join and combine active consumer society with direct democracy – on a world scale.

This comes close to the utopia of a cosmopolitan society which Kant outlined two hundred years ago in his *Perpetual Peace*; he contrasted it with representative democracy, which he opposed as 'despotic'. It is a global nexus of responsibility in which individuals – and not only their representative organizations – can directly take part in political decisions. To be sure, this presupposes purchasing-power and excludes all those who do not have any.

Here lies a further key division: individuals have not at all become directly active; their protest is symbolically mediated through the mass media. Man is a child lost in 'forests of symbols' (Baudelaire). Or, to put it differently, man has to rely upon the symbolic politics of the media. This is true especially in the abstractness and ubiquity of destruction, which is what keeps world risk society going. Here a key political significance attaches to simplifying symbols which can be easily experienced. In these, cultural nerve strings are touched and a sense of alarm created. They are symbols which must be produced, indeed forged, in the open fire of conflict provocation, before the tense and horrified eyes of the television public. The decisive question is who is master of these symbols. Who finds (or invents) symbols which, on the one hand, uncover or highlight the structural character of the problems and, on the other hand, make people capable of action? The latter should be all the more successful, the more straightforward and accessible is the staged symbol, the fewer are the costs of the public protest action for individuals, and the more easily each one can thereby unburden his or her own conscience.

Simplicity means many things. First, there is the question of *transferability*. We are all environmental sinners: just as Shell wanted to sink its oil platform in the sea, 'all of us' itch to throw cola cans out of the car window. It is the everyman situation which makes the Shell case (according to the social construction) so easy to understand – with the crucial difference, to be sure, that the greater the sin, the more enticing the probability of official acquittal. Second, there is the *moral outcry*. 'Those at the top' are given the go-ahead from governments and experts to sink a drilling platform full of oil residue in the North Atlantic, whereas 'we below', for the salvation of the world, are supposed to divide every tea bag in three and dispose of each piece separately in the paper, string or leaf bin. Third, the *political opportunism*. Kohl sided with Greenpeace's action against Shell, but not against the testing of French atomic weapons. For it was not only Shell's market interests, but a game of national power poker that was involved. Fourth, the availability of *simple alternatives*. To hit Shell, one had only to fill up with 'morally good' petrol from one of its competitors. Fifth, *the selling of ecological indulgences*. The boycott gained momentum from the bad conscience of industrial society, because it allowed a kind of self-staged *ego te absolvo* to take place without any costs to the individual.

Global ecological dangers create a horizon of meaning dominated by avoidance, repulsion and salvation, a moral climate that grows more intense with the size of the perceived threat and in which new actors are found and politically allocated to the roles of heroes and scoundrels. To perceive the world as threatened with ecological-industrial self-destruction is to make a universal drama out of morality, religion, fundamentalism, hopelessness, tragedy and tragicomedy (always interwoven with their opposites: salvation, redemption, liberation). In this global stage production, it is left open whether the economy will be the villain of the piece or end up as the heroic saviour. This is precisely the background against which Greenpeace managed to take the stage, with all the cunning of impotence. Greenpeace may be said to pursue a kind of *judo politics*, whose aim is to mobilize the superior strength of environmental sinners against themselves.

In a moment of cynical jollity Josef Stalin once asked, 'How many divisions has the Pope?' The fact is that, in the eyes of decent human opinion, moral challenges are *never* answered by displays of force. The day that Amnesty International takes possession of a machine gun, let alone an atom bomb, its ability to gain a hearing and influence events will be at an end. Institutions with bigger and bigger guns have, in practice, less and less claim to speak on moral issues with the small voice that carries conviction. Here lies the effectiveness of Jonathan Swift's image of *Lilliput*. Stalin failed to see that the military triviality of the Pope's Swiss Guard increases his claim to a hearing, rather than undermining it; while Amnesty International's moral authority is that much greater, just because it is a Lilliputian institution.

To this day, the patterns of our lives are shaped politically by the actions of state authority; yet, morally, rulers of contemporary states are open to outside moral criticism of kinds that have not been widely available since before 1650. Even the most forceful super-powers can no longer ignore the fact. [...] Lilliputian organizations cannot compel immoral rulers to apologize on their knees, as Henry II had to do; but they do subject rulers who refuse to mend their ways to damaging embarrassment in the eyes of the world. If the political image of Modernity was Leviathan, the moral standing of 'national' powers and superpowers will, for the future, be captured in the picture of Lemuel Gulliver, waking from an unthinking sleep, to find himself tethered by innumerable tiny bonds.[5]

Place polygamy: towards globalization in personal life

To appreciate what globalization means when spelt out in people's own lives, there is nothing as useful as a little illustration. A lady who is eighty-four years of age, and who may therefore be called old, lives in...? This is where the story begins. If the local register is to be believed, she has lived without a break for more than thirty years in Tutzing, on Lake Starnberg near Munich. A typical case of (geographical) immobility, one might say. But in fact our old lady flies at least three times a year to Kenya for several weeks or months at a time (usually two months in winter, three to four weeks at Easter, and again in autumn). Where is she 'at home'? In Tutzing? In Kenya? Yes and no. In Kenya she has more friends than in Tutzing and lives in a dense network of Africans and Germans, some of whom have their 'residence' near Hamburg, while others 'come' from Berlin. She also enjoys life more in

Kenya, although she would not like to do without Tutzing altogether. In Africa she is invited to local people's houses and is
generally well looked after. Her well-being in old age is based on
the fact that she 'is someone' in Kenya: she has a 'family' there. In
Tutzing, where she is officially registered, she is a nobody. In her
own words, she lives there 'like a songbird'.

Her acquaintances in Kenya with whom she has a special kind of
'togetherness' also come from Germany, but they have settled into
a life lived between different places and continents. Doris, who is
forty years younger, is married to a (Muslim) Asian in Kenya, but
she keeps going back to Germany to earn her money here or there
(wherever one cares to see it), and to make sure all is well with the
house and garden she owns in the Eifel mountains. She feels well
in both places – which does not mean that the coming and going is
not by now a little too much for her. As to our old lady, 'home-
sickness' has two faces, two voices: it may be called 'Tutzing' as
well as 'Kenya'. Where it carries her depends not least on where
she may already have been back too long.

Is this old lady's life, which spans places in different continents
and binds them together, a disastrous manifestation of dispersal?
No, it is not. For she has not been forced into this transnational way
of life – not even indirectly, as so many are who lead a split life
because of their career. The old lady is in the happy position of not
having to decide either for Tutzing and against Kenya or for Kenya
and against Tutzing. She lives a kind of *place polygamy*: although
Africa and Tutzing appear to exclude each other, *she loves them both*.
Transnational place polygamy, marriage to several places at once,
belonging in different worlds: this is the gateway to globality in
one's own life; it leads to the globalization of biography.

Globalization of biography means that the world's oppositions
occur not only out there but also in the centre of people's lives, in
multicultural marriages and families, at work, in circles of friends,
at school, in the cinema, at the supermarket cheese counter, in
listening to music, eating the evening meal, making love, and so
on. Although people do not will it and are not even aware of it, we
all live more and more in a 'glocal' manner. To grasp the extent of
these changes, it is useful to recall that for a whole century one of
the complaints made by critics of contemporary civilization was
that people are ever more tightly enclosed in the cage of their
highly specialized little world. Now we all suddenly find ourselves
in a situation where the exact opposite is the case. The oppositions
and contradictions of continents, cultures and religions – third and

first world, hole in the ozone layer, mad cow disease, pension reform, disaffection from political parties – arise in lives that have become inextricable from one another. The global does not lurk and threaten out there as the Great All-Encompassing; it noisily fills the innermost space of our own lives. More: it constitutes much of what is distinctively our own in our lives. Our own life is the locus of the glocal. How is this possible?

One's own life is no longer tied to a particular place; it is not a staid, settled life. It is a life 'on the road' (in a direct and transferred sense), a nomadic life, a life in car, aeroplane and train, on the telephone and Internet, a transnational life media-supported and media-stamped. These technologies are everyday means of bridging time and space: they create proximity over distances, and distances within proximity – absence at the same place. To live in one place no longer means to live together, and living together no longer means living in the same place. The central figure of individual life is no longer the *flâneur* but the answering-machine and mailbox: you are there and not there, not answering yet answering automatically, sending and receiving news that is both temporally and spatially mixed, technologically captured and stored from other parts of the world.

The multiple location or transnationality of individual biographies, the globalization of people's lives, is a further reason why national sovereignty is being undermined and a nationally based sociology is becoming obsolete. The association of place with community or society is breaking down. The changing and choosing of place is the model for biographical glocalization.

It should be stressed here that, in view of the opportunities and conflicts of world society, the changing and choosing of place do not always follow subjective decisions. A still fairly mild pressure to change locations comes from people's occupation or career. Brutal physical violence during military conflicts drives thousands of people to different countries and continents, where they then (have to) wander around or, perhaps months or decades later, (have to) return to their 'homeland'. Poverty and hope for a better life lead to immigration that may be legal or illegal, permanent or temporary.[6]

Whether willing or forced, or both, people spread their lives over separate worlds. Polygamous forms of place-living are over-translated biographies – biographies which have to be constantly translated both for oneself and for others, so that they can continue as lives under way. The passage from the first to the second modernity is also the passage from place-monogamous to place-polygamous ways of living.

Place polygamy may, as we have seen, mean many things. It may be acted out within Bavaria between a person's home village and Oberammergau, or it may involve continual crossing between cultures (among third-generation German-Turkish youth, for example) or between continents (the Vietnamese in the former GDR and now Berlin). The continents of the world may also be experienced and suffered in *one* global place (London, for example). It is therefore necessary to draw some distinctions.

'Globalization of biography' refers not just to any kind of multiple location, but only to that *multilocation* which involves crossing the borders of separate worlds (nations, religions, cultures, skin colours, continents, etc.), and whose oppositions must or may lodge in a single life. For the notion that many lives in one *must* mean despair and impossibly high demands is a legend that place-monogamists use to shield themselves from the impositions of place-polygamists.

If we are to understand the social figure of a globalization of personal life, we must focus on the oppositions involved in stretching between different places. This requires, among other things, that mobility should be understood in a new way. Mobility in the old sense – mobility of a single living or acting unit (family, couple or individual) between two places (points) in the social hierarchy or landscape – has been losing or changing its significance. What is coming to the fore is the *inner* mobility of an individual's own life, for which coming and going, being both here and there across frontiers at the same time, has become the normal thing. Thus, it is possible to be immobile according to official registration statistics, and yet to live a non-settled existence in several places at once. (This should be clearly distinguished from the *outer* mobility of such exceptional occurrences as a house move, a change of job, divorce, forced flight, emigration, etc.) Inner mobility is no longer the exception but the rule, not something alien but something familiar, constantly occurring in many different forms. One could say it has become second nature to keep having to 'find one's place', between different places each with their special social demands. Inner mobility and multilocation – transnational, transcontinental, transreligious, transethnic, in biographical cross-section and in the longitudinal section of life – are two sides of the same thing. Inner, as opposed to outer, mobility thus denotes the extent of mental and physical mobility that is necessary or desirable to master everyday life between different worlds. This also expresses the *limits* of inner mobility, which are set not only by the (financial) difficulties of socially coordinating and mastering everyday life, but also by old age, illness, disability, and so on.

These different worlds are potentially present at a single place (by virtue of information, consumption, social, cultural and religious oppositions), dependent on the available sources of information, the variety of cross-cultural relations, migration, legislation pertaining to aliens, etc. In other words, the idea that one lives in a single, self-enclosed place can everywhere be seen to be false.[7]

Maarten Hajer, alluding to U. Hannerz, speaks of a 'transnationalization of place'.

> Transnationalization establishes new connections between cultures, people and places, thereby altering our everyday environment. Not only does it bring scarcely known products into our supermarkets (such as ciabatta or pitta bread) or signs and symbols into our cities (Chinese and Japanese writing or Islamic music, for example); but new groups and people (Africans, Bosnians, Croats, Poles and Russians, as well as Japanese and Americans) also become more strongly present in those cities and for a time affect how they are perceived by many citizens. In the big cities, moreover, transnationalization visibly influences the new culture of the second modernity – for example, in the form of Islamic disco music, culinary hybrids (so-called *cuisine sauvage*), world music performances, and Euro-Asian, Afro-European or Afro-Caribbean children.[8]

But when the concept of place is itself ambiguous, what does multilocation or transnationality of one's own life actually mean? If my own life is stretched over several places, it may mean that it takes place in *common or general space*: for example, in airports, hotels and restaurants which are everywhere more or less the same and therefore placeless, and which make the question 'Who am I?' ultimately unanswerable. Or (just to take the opposite extreme) multilocation may mean that one keeps falling in love with and marrying what is different in places, in their faces and histories. In this way, places become new opportunities for discovering and testing out particular aspects of oneself. To what extent is the place 'my place', and 'my place' my own life? How are the different places related to one another in the imaginary map of 'my world', and in what sense are they 'significant places' in the longitudinal and cross-section of my own life?[9]

Multilocation – in relation to the grand sociological narratives – does not therefore mean either emancipation or non-emancipation, anomie or non-anomie, an automatic 'cosmopolitan vision' or a new fundamentalism, indiscriminateness or alarmism. Nor does it mean defamation (by equating Islam, fundamentalism and violence, for example). What it does mean is something new, about which one may be or become curious, as one does about new things, in order to decipher its (view of the) world.

> There we encounter people with exotic-sounding names, unfamiliar appearances, different hair and skin colours, which all evoke in us associations with faraway lands and the Orient. Then they suddenly reply in Bavarian or Swabian dialect, and it turns out that they grew up in the Kreuzberg district of Berlin or in Duisburg. In short, they turn our expectations right around: they place our images of normality in question.
>
> As we read in a novel of Kureishi's: 'Everyone looks at you and thinks: what a nice little Indian boy, how exotic! How exciting! What tales of aunties and elephants we'll get to hear from him!' – until it transpires that the Indian boy is from the London suburb of Orpington and has never even been on a visit to India. The world then seems to have gone crazy. Nothing is as it seems. Who is what? Who is who?
>
> Similar stories can be told from Germany.
>
> 'Well now, Herr Kayanka. So you're a private detective. Interesting name that – Kayanka.'
>
> 'Not so much interesting as Turkish.'
>
> 'Ah!'
>
> The smile becomes even sweeter, the eye slits hardly larger than razor blades.
>
> 'Turkish. A Turkish private detective? So now there's one of everything. And how come you speak such good German, if I may presume to ask?'
>
> 'Because I never learnt any other language. My parents died young and I grew up in a German family.'
>
> 'But you are Turkish – I mean...'
>
> 'I have a German passport, if that puts your mind at rest.' (J. Arjouni, *Ein Mann, ein Mord*, Zurich 1991).[10]

On the possibility of inter-cultural critique

A cartoon shows the Spanish conquistadors entering the New World with glittering weapons. 'We have come to you,' says the balloon, 'to speak with you of God, civilization and truth.' And a group of puzzled-looking natives answer: 'But of course: what do you want to know?'

It has often been described, to little enough effect, how events then led and still lead to bloodbaths. But what is funny about this scene? The comedy comes from the mutual *mis*understanding of the 'encounter'. Western imperialism bristling with arms disguises its missionary zeal beneath the phrasemongering of 'cross-cultural dialogue'. The conquered natives naively misunderstand, and seek to represent the situation as one of proffered dialogue, but they are to be fattened like Christmas geese with foreign certitudes and then slaughtered.

The bitterness of the comedy lies in the fact that the observer knows *more* than the situation reveals, and that the cartoonist plays with that knowledge. The onlooker is aware of what really lies ahead. He knows what ravages and bloodbaths came into the world through the blindness to strangers which was built into those certainties of theirs. The laughter dies away amid the tragedy of the situation – a tragedy that has jinxed the world right down to the present day. Tragedy and comedy are the two sides of a cross-cultural 'dialogue' that has repeatedly failed.

This being so, we need to ask whether anything like cross-cultural criticism is ever possible. Or, more naively: *How* will it become possible?

To make sure we have got the question right, we shall first interrogate the classics of tolerance and misunderstanding (Nietzsche and Lessing), and then try to build some bridges between the opposing camps of (postmodern) contextualism and (Enlightenment) universalism.

'That wisdom full of pranks'

There is certainly the postmodern Nietzsche, who merrily shatters certainties by exposing the egoistical content of morality, and who preaches immoralism, irresponsibility and self-interest. But there is also the ironical Enlightenment Nietzsche, perhaps even the still-to-be-discovered founder of one such Enlightenment. And he knew of the wisdom of laughter, which he called 'that wisdom full of pranks': 'the joyful kind of seriousness and that wisdom full of pranks'.[11]

Nietzsche replaces sympathy or compassion [*Mit-Leiden*] with laughing together [*Mit-Lachen*]. For him, the destruction of values is evidently not an end in itself; it is supposed to create the space for rejoicing and laughing together in a process of cross-cultural (and 'cross-truth') dialogue – through others whose masks one has pulled on, through the masks one has oneself become and sees with the eyes of others, and so on. Thus, the globality that Nietzsche sees before his eyes does not suddenly arise all at once, but includes centuries of living with and against one another. But what is the morality of 'glocal' living in Nietzsche's ironical vision?

It is easier to say what it is *not*. It is neither a moral *tabula rasa* nor conventional morality. It assumes that the absolutist moralities of separate worlds will be broken up – not so that there should be nothing, but so that there is space for a simultaneous *reduction* and *expansion* of moral standards and demands. 'Hence a morality of *testing*, of *giving* oneself a goal.'[12]

'That wisdom full of pranks', simplified and methodically applied, is for Nietzsche expressed in a twofold *démarche*. On the one hand, he makes the case for an *individualization of ideals*: individuals become legislators, but only of *themselves*. Individualization thus accomplishes, in the realm of morality, the greatest possible reduction of standards. They are valid for me, only for me. Morality thus becomes possible as self-legislation and *only* self-legislation.

This does not open the door wide to the relativist principle of 'let everyone do as they please'. Nietzsche's intention is quite the opposite: for he senses that tolerance which remains within its own moral certainty is never more than a *chattering* tolerance, the tolerance of 'we have come to speak with you of God, civilization and truth' in that conquistador balloon. Tolerance must be radically conceived and practised in two directions at once: reduction of one's own sovereign moral territory in order to seek cross-cultural dialogue with other and others' truths.

The individualization of morality, then, does not spring from any egoistical motive. Rather, it opens up the opportunity for a *global* morality of tolerance. This makes possible not only dialogue but a 'hybrid' such as cross-cultural criticism. Self-legislation, in this double sense of limitation and expansion, makes people capable of criticism, capable of conflict.

For Nietzsche, self-limitation opens our eyes to legislation for ourselves alone, perhaps freed of the circularity of enemy-images. It means that contact with the certainties of others can take place in an experimental sphere of experience and action. Nietzsche's answer to the question of how cross-cultural criticism is possible may with great simplification be expressed as follows. Only self-legislation *and* self-questioning can together open us up and strengthen us for the challenges of international life.

Self-legislation *without* self-questioning leads to intolerance, ethnocentrism, egocentrism; and self-questioning *without* self-legislation leads to weakening and capitulation in face of the narrowness of the world.

This contradiction is resolved in what Nietzsche calls 'a morality of *testing*, of *giving* oneself a goal'. The individualization of ideals reduces *and* enlarges the territory of morality, because in this way the moral laws of others can be experienced and desired as an *enrichment* of one's own life. 'We [...] want to become those we are – human beings who are new, unique, incomparable, who give themselves laws, who create themselves.'[13] The counter-question is immediately to hand. What happens if those who give laws only to themselves bash one another's heads in?

In many respects, a similar answer can be found in Lessing, who deals with the question of mutually exclusive certainties, especially in his play *Nathan the Wise*. It already starts from the premiss that the 'wisdom' of Nathan the Wise chiefly consists in a fractured relationship to his own supposed wisdom, as to all pompous idealisms which make people blind to the world. When Sultan Saladin asks him: 'You are called Nathan the Wise?', he answers 'No.' And on the Sultan's retort: 'By yourself, Oh no, but by the people,' he allows: 'Maybe; the people.' Then follows a discussion of the dubious honour of being called 'wise' by the people.

Today, perhaps, we would say that Nathan is an early 'pragmatist' in matters of belief and truth. He wants to see, feel and hold what follows from the words that often sit so proudly on the lips. 'We have come to speak with you of God, civilization and truth.' – 'Of course: what do you want to know?' That moral claptrap was repulsive to Nathan, whose attitude to it was one of irony.

At first Nathan suspects an ambush in the Sultan's startling question: 'tell me as to a friend, / What faith, what law, have satisfied you best.' To gain time, he tells the famous parable of the ring, which is thus conceived *not* as a reply but as an escape.

The ring in the parable symbolizes election. It always passes down from the father to his most beloved son – until one father, who loves and esteems all his three sons alike, has two more rings made of just the same beauty and value so that he will not have to disappoint any of his sons. But since each thinks he is in possession of the true ring and is therefore the chosen one, a public dispute soon erupts. 'Thus spake the Judge: Bring me the father here / To witness; I will hear him; and if not / Leave then my judgement seat. Think you this chair / Is set for reading of riddles?'[14]

The necessity of choosing between the mutually exclusive certainties of the Christian, Jewish and Muslim religions is given a paradoxical solution: none at all, but also two. The judge does not give a ruling: he calls on the suppliants to think and act for themselves. At the same time, he gives the truth-seekers a criterion to take on their way. According to his judgement, the only possible proof of their 'election' is in *the fruits of what they do*. Activity, conflict, strife and proving oneself will increase the number of signs, but only those which point to the truth. Here too – as in Nietzsche – the claim to truth is withdrawn, both to defuse the world of contradictory certainties *and* to open up space for creative activity.

Simply put, Lessing's answer is to draw a distinction that cannot be written too large: the distinction between *certainty* and *truth*. Certainty, in the terms of the parable, is to *possess* the father's *only* ring; truth is the uncertainty about which of the three rings is 'genuine'. This uncertainty of truth is irrevocable. In certainty, all doubt falls away. In truth, by contrast, doubt lives and is perhaps in command.

The ring in the parable bestows the quality of being especially loved. Truth must earn its quality of being true. 'To be especially loved' (recognition of one's actions in other people's eyes) becomes the means of proving to oneself and others the native power of the ring. So does doubt about the truth release activity which must prove itself. It is thinking and doing for oneself, not having something, which opens up possibilities and fashions new spaces.

Thus alongside Lessing's gentle farewell to certainty, more plaintive than ironic, one finds the advice that not to have certainty wins people over to other people and their truths. Lessing too combines the maxim of self-limitation – acceptance that there are more than one contradictory truths or realities – with a firm attachment to the ring as token of multiple election. In other words, universalist and relativist principles are so intertwined that the *fight* for truth becomes the precondition of socially valuable action.

Contextual universalism

Nietzsche and Lessing employ different, even radically different, arguments, yet they point in the same direction. They are *not* prepared – as we would say today – to give up either universalist principles or relativist principles. Universalism has the disadvantage that one's own standpoint is thrust upon others, but the advantage that others are involved and taken seriously. It is important to distinguish between a universalist and a *totalizing* (or, in the extreme, *totalitarian*) standpoint. Nietzsche understands that a universalist standpoint is perfectly compatible with self-limiting self-legislation, and he also, like Lessing, knows about the distinction between truth and certainty. Neither can be said of totalizing tendencies, in which a historically murky picture of one's own morality becomes the yardstick for everyone.

On the other hand, relativism and *contextual* thinking are indispensable, because they sharpen our *respect for cultural difference* and make a change of perspective both attractive and necessary.

Faced with the choice between universalism and contextualism (relativism), both Nietzsche and Lessing reject the Either-Or and look for what I call inclusive distinctions. I would like to take up this struggle for an *and* – for a combination of universalism *and* contextualism (relativism) – and to carry it further by applying the distinction to itself.

What we have, then, is a table made up of four fields: *universalist universalism* (UU), *universalist contextualism* or relativism (UC), *contextual universalism* (CU), and *contextual contextualism* or relativism (CC). Since the fourth position is very similar in content to the third, the following account will only elucidate (with shafts of light) the first three positions.

The first two positions, UU and UC, have *totalizing* features in varying degrees. This is true, for instance, of the old Enlightenment, which spoke of *men* (or in German, of gender-neutral *Menschen*), when what it meant were *white males with a high level of education*. Even the claims of scientists that their methods can express the one true nature or reality have become ridiculous.

In another way, however, this is also true of *totalizing contextualism* (or *relativism*). With quite different arguments, but with similar results, a change of perspective is rejected on the simple grounds that it is impossible. For if everything is relative (let us return here to our earlier example), the conquerors have their point of view and the conquered have theirs; the cartoonist observing the scene and those who look at his cartoon also have points of view of their own. More or less unbridgeable chasms yawn between all of them. In short, all are simply what they are.

The unintended irony of the incommensurability thesis is that it is the spitting image of an *essentialist* view of the world. It leads (astray) to a postmodern quasi-essentialism, which is like the genuine article in insisting that things just have to be accepted as they are.

Perhaps it is useful, therefore, to think not only of a self-limitation of one's own moral principles, but also of a self-limitation of one's own *relativism*. In the end, absolutized contextualism and absolutized universalism are similarly *blind* to the truths of others. The one is blocked by the enemy-image inherent in its own certainty, the other by the supposed impossibility of ever understanding another's standpoint.

Universalist contextualism (relativism) is a fancy way of saying *non-interference*. Here prevails the perpetual (non-)peace of perpetual relativism. A wish to be left, and to leave others, in peace is justified by arguing that the trenches between cultures can never be crossed, that dialogue only ever reflects back one's own certainties. Admittedly that is a polemical way of putting it – it may also be wrong so far as motives are concerned. But in its *results*, the conjecture of incommensurability comes down to an a priori pact of non-interference between cultures, and an assertion of the impossibility of dialogue or of any kind of change in perspective. It is precisely this which is the important aspect: the affirmation of exclusive standpoints *without* trial and error, as a matter of principle, with no reference to experience, is itself, so to speak, anti-contextualist. I would like to take this turning aside from experience as an opportunity to formulate a counter-position, one which may be called *contextual universalism*. For it may be thought of and developed precisely as a mirror image.

Contextual universalism starts from the opposite case – namely, that *non*-interference is *im*possible. For it contends that we are living in the age of homogeneity, in a global era. Any attempt to keep out of it, to escape into an illusion of separate worlds, is grotesque and unintentionally comical. The world *is* a caricature of dialogue (or non-dialogue), whose participants unavoidably talk at cross-purposes with one another. To cover this up in well-meaning rhetoric about learning from one another is not very helpful, but nor is it at all necessary so long as one builds upon the *creative power of misunderstanding*.[15]

There is no reason to complain here about false alternatives. The thesis in opposition to the conjecture of incommensurability is not that a *dialogue* does take place. It is only that there are no separate worlds. There is the riotous profusion of a globally disarticulated context, in the face of which a retreat into non-dialogue appears *idyllic*.

Since a non-interference pact is ruled out, an acceptance of glocal living comes into the picture. In this perspective, the false joys of incommensurability appear as illusory escapes from the trap of cross-cultural misunderstanding into which the world has fallen. What is up for debate is the *how*, not the whether, of mutual interference and conflicting forms of involvement.

It is possible to counterpose the two principles without any illusion, indeed with the sceptical undertone rightly expressed in the incommensurability thesis. Absolute contextualism insists: Just leave me alone! – not because any disturbance is forbidden, but because it is anyway excluded by the gulf of incomparability. By contrast, contextual universalism maintains that there is no escape from the unrest of mutual interference between exclusive certainties. To what extent can there be perspectival change, dialogue, talking at cross-purposes, laughter and conflicts? To what extent are these possible and necessary, or meaningless and absurd, or all of these things at once? I can know the answer to this question only *after* I have taken the relevant step. The essential difference between the two principles, therefore, is not that the first denies any through-route while the second affirms it, but that the first rules it out without even trying, while the second wrestles with the unavoidable *experience* of a test. (Whatever the point of view, both may look, or become, decidedly odd.)

In the view of contextual universalism, then, incommensurability signifies neither *pre-established ignorance*; nor the *self-righteousness* that is a paradoxical result of absolutized relativism; nor the presumed *certainty*, without any *trial* or *experience*, that an exchange of perspectives and arguments would be meaningless. Absolute relativism means that I do not have to open my sanctuary to anyone else, or expose myself to their criticism. For contextual universalism, the question is: How can I *learn to laugh* at the objects in my own sanctuary, while passing through the sanctuaries of others?

The first attempt at inclusive distinction comes down to a direct integration of the contextual into the concept of the universal. This makes invalid the alternative: *either* a single universalism *or* no universalism. But the possibility arises that there are *my* universalism and *your* universalism, many universalisms – *plural* universalism. Once the absolutist claims of universalism are broken down, it can be seen that this does not leave *no sacred objects at all* but (as in Nietzsche's thought) self-limitation to *my* sacred objects – which raises in turn the question of the universalism of *others*. An example may serve to clarify this.

Human rights should not be brought under the principle of universalist universalism: in other words, they do not have to apply everywhere on earth in the form in which they were *invented* in the West, nor is it true that *only* the West asserts and defends rights that are inalienable for all men and women. It is well known that the idea of human rights can also be found in other cultures, traditions and religions, where their significance may sometimes complement, sometimes subtract from the concept as understood in the West. Different *versions* of human rights even exist in the various parts of Europe. In the Scandinavian countries, for example, economic rights are counted among basic rights, whereas in the post-communist countries of Central and Eastern Europe civil and political rights are often highly valued by the population but not by the government. Demands originating in other regions of the world point to yet another understanding of rights. Thus, there is an *African Charter on Human and Peoples' Rights*.

> This reflects what has been considered a specifically African concept of human rights, developed from the norms of traditional African societies and based upon two important principles – communitarianism, which rejects the individualism of the western model, and decision-making through consensual procedures, which obviates the need for competitive elections. These principles are central to claims of cultural relativism and have relevance beyond Africa.[16]

Curiosity about other conceptions and traditions of human rights does not, as universalist universalism fears, lead to abandonment of the idea of equal rights for all. 'Only now', we might say, is the competition beginning between cultures, nations, states and religions, to decide which conceptions of human rights are most *helpful* to human beings. And 'dialogue' about this, jinxed though it may be, is also beginning.

What is coming to an end is the great silence of the various priests of universalism, on their heights of self-righteousness. To assert no more than one's own universalism is not necessarily to leave other universalisms just as they are; it does not entail a mutual hands-off agreement. On the contrary: only a renunciation of claims that my version of human rights is the only one enables it to contend for validity alongside other versions.

Contextual universalism does not oblige anyone, in the name of some misguided relativism, to accept human rights violations in other cultures and countries. But nor does it sanction invasion of other authorities – to protect minorities from persecution, for example. It asks: What conceptions of human rights, and what human rights groups, are there in the countries where human rights are being grossly violated? How do *they* judge what is happening in their country, from their point of view and with their knowledge of human rights? And how do their interpretations relate to our (my) hypotheses about human rights which are universally applicable (including in the country in question)?

But reversion to a contextual (our, my, Western) version of universal human rights is not by any means tantamount to moral-political capitulation before the bestialities of the twentieth century. Indeed, it actually presupposes interference in conflicts over human rights and human rights violations in other cultures and countries.

Contextual universalism implies that the things we hold most sacred must be opened to criticism by others. The *sacrilege of polytheism* must be committed in the cause of universalism, and first of all with regard to oneself. To use the language of Lessing, the step from *certainty* to *truth* – at once philosophical, moral and political – must be consciously taken in the field of universalism. In the imaginative world of many universalisms, perhaps heartfelt laughter will one day ring out at the foolish human presumptuousness of universal certainty.

3

Contours of World Society: Rival Perspectives

We have now gathered, compared and analysed enough arguments to take up our thematic question once more. How should *globality*, *globalization* and *globalism* be distinguished from one another?

Globalization lays the stress upon a transnational process, in the dimensions we have considered above.

1 It refers to intensification of transnational spaces, events, problems, conflicts and biographies.

2 This tendency – contrary to everything the word 'global' suggests – should not be understood either as linear or as 'total' or 'all-encompassing'. Rather, it should be thought of as only *contingent* and *dialectical* – as *glocal*. This will become clearer if the conceptual figure of 'inclusive distinction or opposition' is employed as the underlying principle of biography, identity and organization.

3 It then becomes necessary to consider the *degree*, *density* and *extent* of globalization/localization in the various dimensions. Thus, the manifestations of glocalization can and must be *empirically* investigated.

The concept *globality* is aimed at a stronger reality claim: it signifies – ultimately – *world society* as an *irrevocable* fact. This 'world society' should be conceived as:

- *multidimensional,*
- *polycentric,*

- *contingent* and
- *political*.

The question should be raised in the sense given to it by cultural theory. In which forms and forums is world society lived, experienced, socially perceived and practised – in such a way as to become *actual*? Roland Robertson was the first to take, as an indicator of reflexive world society, the extent to which people are conscious of living in the world as *one* place. A. Nassehi gives a similar definition:

> One should speak of world society when global players see each other as *differently related to one and the same world*, and this becomes reflexive. World society is then – in accordance with the Thomas theorem – a world horizon which opens up when it proves itself in communication to be real. Only against this background is it possible to decode as a *world social phenomenon* not only the exploitation of labour in a different part of the world, but also the social-romantic ethno-eclecticism of educated Westerners in need of philosophical and touristic recuperation. In this sense, the discovery of America, the Crusades and the colonial policy of the nineteenth century were *not* world social events.[1]

To be distinguished from globalization and globality is a further concept, *globalism*, which refers to the neoliberal ideology of world-market domination. An attempted critique of globalism will be made in Part II of this book. But we should first amplify the thesis of the irrevocability of world society, by briefly outlining and comparing six partly competing, partly complementary perspectives. We shall do this under the following headings:

1 Third cultures or global civil society?
2 Cosmopolitan democracy
3 Capitalist world society
4 World risk society
5 Global society without democratic politics
6 Prospects for a transnational state

Third cultures or global civil society?

In his *Perpetual Peace*, Kant developed the argument that democracies are never ultimately possible in the *isolated* form of a single society or state, but only in the form of cosmopolitan society. Instead of the self-government of the many just being a matter of their thinking and acting for themselves, it presupposes (a) *self-experience of global civil society* and (b) *basic legal relationships that are universally valid*.

If 'world society' is thus to be linked to the self-experience of world society, the question must be asked whether there can be such a thing as global memory resulting from separate experiences and dangers. Contexts of transnational experience are historical in their emergence and continued existence – for example, as a result of trade relations, migration-flows, slavery, conquest, wars, imperialism or colonialism. A. D. Smith, in particular, has disputed any idea that colonial history can become the content of global culture and identity.

> Unlike national cultures, a global culture is essentially memoryless. Where the 'nation' can be constructed so as to draw upon and receive latent popular experiences and needs, a 'global culture' answers to no living needs, no identity-in-the-making. [...] There are no 'world memories' that can be used to *unite* humanity; the most global experiences to date – colonialism and the World Wars – can only serve to remind us of our historic cleavages.[2]

J. N. Pieterse answers this as follows:

> If conflict, conquest and repression would *only* divide people, then nations themselves would merely be artefacts of division for they too were mostly born out of conflict. Likewise, on the larger canvas, it would be shallow and erroneous to argue that the experiences of conflict merely divide humanity: they also unite humankind, even if in painful ways and producing an ambivalent kind of unity. Unity emerging out of antagonism and conflict is the a, b, c of dialectics. [...] A conflictual unity bonded by common political and cultural experiences, including the experience of domination, has been part of the make-up of hybrid postcolonial cultures. Thus the former British Empire remains in many ways a unitary space featuring a common language, common elements in legal and political systems, infrastructure, traffic rules, an imperial architecture which is in many ways the same in India as in South Africa, along with the legacy of the Commonwealth.[3]

If experience of world society is an essential feature of world society, then multicultural society is not a phantom of the brain but a global reality. One can neither choose it nor opt out of it. It does not automatically lead to tolerance, but can also trigger seclusion and xenophobia. If the ambivalences of world society burst into conflict at certain places, this does not mean the collapse of 'multi-cultural social experiments' and may even mark the beginning of a new epoch in which transnational and transcultural ways of living will be the norm. A people that blots out these realities and con-tinues to think of itself and others in terms of monolithic national cultures will find it difficult to cope with the quite normal confu-sion of world society.

> How do we come to terms with phenomena such as Thai boxing by Moroccan girls in Amsterdam, Asian rap in London, Irish bagels, Chinese tacos and Mardi Gras Indians in the United States, or 'Mexican schoolgirls dressed in Greek togas dancing in the style of Isadora Duncan' [Rowe and Schelling]? How do we interpret Peter Brook directing the *Mahabharata*, or Ariane Mnouchkine staging a Shakespeare play in Japanese Kabuki style for a Paris audience in the Théâtre Soleil? Cultural experiences, past or present, have not been simply moving in the direction of cultural uniformity and standardization. This is not to say that the notion of global cultural synchronization is irrelevant – on the contrary – but it is fundamen-tally incomplete. It overlooks the countercurrents – the impact non-Western cultures have been making on the West. It downplays the ambivalence of the globalizing momentum and ignores the role of local reception of Western culture – for example, the indigenization of Western elements. It fails to see the influence that non-Western cultures have been exercising on one another. It has no room for crossover culture – as in the development of 'third cultures' such as world music. It overrates the homogeneity of Western culture and overlooks the fact that many of the standards exported by the West and its cultural industries themselves turn out to be of culturally mixed character if we examine their cultural lineages. Centuries of North–South cultural osmosis have resulted in an intercontinental crossover culture. European and Western culture are *part* of this global mélange. This is an obvious case if we reckon that Europe until the fourteenth century was invariably the recipient of cultural influences from 'the Orient'. The hegemony of the West dates only from very recent times, from around 1800, and, arguably, from industrialization.[4]

Perhaps it is no accident that, for the overwhelming majority of people today, the experience of a 'common global destiny' first appears as an *experience of danger* – in discussions of 'mobile poverty' or the 'population explosion', in events such as the Chernobyl nuclear disaster, news items about toxins in food, air or water, or an announcement that their own company intends to create new jobs in other parts of the world. In these cases too, however, people have concrete experience that 'world society' is not something happening 'out there' but is affecting the foundations of their own lives. In other words, the reality and power of people's experience of world society is also proven in the ways in which they try to fend it off.

Martin Shaw goes a crucial step further. For him, 'experience' of global civil society means, first, *self-perception* (through the mass media) and, second, its possible *relevance to behaviour*. He therefore empirically investigates the extent to which a global civil society has actually taken shape, by reviewing the wars since the end of the East–West conflict and their significance for the actions of distant others (military intervention by the UN or other states). Formerly, Shaw argues, wars and combatants were restricted to the place where violence was exercised; epochal wars were few and far between. Today and in the future, however, potential or actual involvement through the mass media means that wars take place worldwide. Global civil society is becoming a global viewing society. In a sense wars thus lose their spatial location and, through their telegenic (re-)presentation, become *political crises* in which questions of justice and intervention must also be publicly discussed and decided in the far-off centres of global civil society.

> We therefore have to ask whether post-Cold War crises are genuinely *global* political crises and, if so, what makes them such? The case rests on how far they are perceived to have global ramifications and whether intervention from outside the region of conflict, by the great powers or the United Nations, has taken place or become a serious possibility. Clearly, those crises which can genuinely be considered global are crises of a different order from the world wars or the superpower confrontations during the Cold War. It does seem appropriate, however, to consider some at least of the new crises in this light. Why have some wars, such as those in Bosnia and Rwanda, been considered as globally significant? It is not obvious that they are qualitatively different from other wars, such as Armenia-Azerbaijan and the civil war in Angola. These too have involved huge death tolls and massive clearances of populations. The principal difference seems to be that some wars have been widely *perceived* to involve enormous suffering and violations of

human rights, in disregard of principles avowed by the 'international community', and that this perception has been fostered by extensive global media coverage. Large-scale suffering and violations of human rights have been present in many other cases; perceptions of them have had, however, much less currency, and the obvious explanation is the relative weakness of coverage.

We may thus speak of a *media generation and construction* of the global significance of a local military conflict, which activates both global civil society *and* the global dimension of the conflict.

We may note two new criteria for global political crises. Global crises may still be constituted, as was the Gulf War for the most part, by traditional criteria of conflicts of interests directly or indirectly involving major powers and areas of the international system. They may also be constituted, however, even where these are wholly or largely lacking, if there is a world-wide *perception* of a large-scale violation of human life and globally legitimate principles that is largely dependent on media coverage obtained. The existence of a global crisis can be confirmed by the occurrence of, or existence of significant pressure for, internationally legitimate *intervention* to resolve it.

In reality, traditional and new models of global political crises are not alternatives but indicate poles on a spectrum. Each crisis combines traditional and new aspects in different proportions. Although Bosnia and Angola, for example, no longer represent the sorts of geographical security interests for great powers which they did during the Cold War (which is, ironically, a reason for the eruption of new conflicts), there are still broad great-power interests in the regional security of the Balkans and southern Africa. Conversely the Gulf, the only post-Cold War war to appear as a pure inter-state conflict, entailed immense civil conflicts and human tragedies. The mediation of these in global communications quite changed the war's initial character and historic significance. We may conclude that threats to civil communities and their mediation are key aspects not merely of one kind of crisis but of contemporary global crises in general.

This shift in the definition of global political crises brings it closer to a broader concept of global crises in a social and humanitarian sense, to include famine, poverty, repression, natural disasters, epidemics and environmental catastrophes. Since these are most commonly produced or exacerbated by political crises, and especially wars, such a shift would seem to be appropriate. Indeed there may be a case for seeing social crises largely as aspects of political crises. Perceptions of humanitarian crises may be changing: for example, whereas in the 1970s and 1980s famine was often understood as a product of drought, now media coverage has publicized its roots in wars.[5]

Cosmopolitan democracy

Alongside the self-experience of civil society, transnationally applicable basic rights provide the foundation of a cosmopolitan democracy. As far as the applicability of basic rights is concerned, what matters in Kant's view is a gradual introduction of rights between citizens of different nationalities, and thus ultimately the establishment of cosmopolitan rights for all. This includes a gradual introduction of the content of various political and social rights into the life of individual countries. Civilization is protected against barbarism (never more than provisionally) only when the relationship expressed in basic rights applies *globally*.[6]

A paradox arises here which is still today an obstacle to any debate. A guarantee of basic rights, it would seem, presupposes the national state. So how is it possible to establish and secure a cosmopolitan legal relationship between different states and citizens which reduces the importance of the national state as guarantor, without at the same time becoming lost in the false alternative of either striving for a world state (to take the place of national states) or placing basic rights in a space without laws or states?

In the defence of human rights, a variety of players compete, cooperate and conflict with one another – intergovernmental organizations such as agencies of the United Nations, individual states acting alone or together with other states or non-governmental organizations, and regional unions of one kind or another. Relations between these state or non-state players and ordinary individuals who are bearers of the rights in question may be described by means of one of three models: a realist model, an internationalist model, or a cosmopolitan model.

> The realist, state-centric model emphasizes the primacy, and sovereignty, of states. Hence, for realists, the rights of individuals are a matter of domestic jurisdiction and the role of intergovernmental organizations and NGOs is, at best, advisory. In terms of interstate relationships, the exigencies of sovereignty prohibit interference in the domestic affairs of other states, while foreign policy should be informed by self-interest rather than considerations of morality. Hence decisions to provide financial assistance, or indeed torture

equipment, should be based upon the single criterion of advantage to the supplier.

A modification of the realist view is provided by the internationalist model. Here states continue to occupy a central role and retain primary responsibility for individual rights. Nevertheless their actions are influenced, and to some extent modified, by an evolving consensus on human rights norms. Intergovernmental organizations and NGOs are capable of playing a significant role, and in some circumstances do so, but their capacity for effective action remains conditional upon the cooperation of states. Thus the influence of the UN Commission on Human Rights or of Amnesty International is considerably greater in Canada than in China or, indeed, the United Kingdom.

The third model might be labelled cosmopolitan. Here the individual is at the centre of analysis, and a direct relationship is posited between individuals and intergovernmental organizations and NGOs. Thus the primacy of the state in global politics is increasingly challenged, both from below and above, to the extent that the development of a global civil society is presaged. Cosmopolitans would emphasize the development of the UN human rights machinery since the end of the Cold War as well as the proliferation in number, and growth in membership, of human rights and other NGOs during the same period.[7]

The key transnational guarantee of basic rights is not a cross-cultural consensus but the development of cooperative procedures and relations of dependence. The partly codified, partly non-codified procedures in which transnational links – a dense multidimensional network of mutual bonds and duties – are initiated, negotiated and cultivated: this is what is supposed to underpin the idea of *cosmopolitan democracy* and to facilitate its realization. David Held has outlined as follows this vision of the future:[8]

1 The global order is made concrete in multiple, overlapping power networks, which encompass human bodies, welfare, culture, voluntary organizations, the economy, international ties of dependence, and organized violence. The scope for cosmopolitan democracy arises out of these varied networks, out of a multidimensional balance of power among nations, organizations and people.

2 All groups and organizations claim a relative autonomy, which is expressed in certain rights and duties. This pattern of what is permitted and forbidden must be tied together in *funda-*

mental principles of cosmopolitan democratic law, which then need to be spelt out individually for the fields of action of the social, the economic and the political.

3 These legal principles are legitimated and guaranteed by *transnationally and locally articulated parliaments and courts* – the model here being the European Parliament and the European Court of Justice – which would also have to be established in the transnational spaces of South America, Asia and Africa.

4 National states cede parts of their power and sovereignty to transnational institutions and organizations, and develop a new understanding of themselves as nodal points and coordinators of transnational dependence.

5 Individuals may come to belong to different national and transnational power areas, and thus exercise rights to participation and self-determination from the local up to the global level.

6 Public money for everyone – regardless of whether they are involved in the private sector, domestic labour or public civil employment; this guarantees the exercise of political freedom.

As to its sociological realism, this appears all fine and rosy – but no more than that. Whether such a development is supported or blocked and by which real powers and tendencies, what contradictions and paradoxes are inherent in this picture-book vision of cosmopolitan democracy, will be left to one side for the moment. I remember that, already at the beginning of the nineteenth century, Auguste Comte 'refuted' militant imperialism – by its own measure of rationality, so to speak – as economically unprofitable, but then came the collectively willed and organized madness of imperialism, colonialism, two world wars, the Holocaust, the Stalinist gulag. One can but *hope* that this normative vision will not similarly be torn apart and overwhelmed by its own contradictions and adversaries. But for social science and politics, hope is too little.

A number of questions will take us somewhat further. What contradictions are to be found in this hope? Which political-social landslides and erosions are likely to crush or advance it? Let us now look at these, again in rather summary fashion.

Capitalist world society

Many neo-Marxists will consider the idea of cosmopolitan democracy to be devoid of reality, mainly on the grounds that it jumbles up ethics and power. The question of a world horizon of values and ideas, it is argued, fails to recognize the transnational relations of economic power which become aggravated through processes of economic globalization. Since the end of the Cold War and the integration of the Communist power bloc into the world market, basic aspects of the capitalist dynamic that were 'covered up' in Western welfare capitalism have emerged in a sharper form. This whole conceptual approach may be further considered in the following seven steps and theorems.

(1)   *Transnational integration and national disintegration are simultaneous with each other.* In the triumphal march of the world market, the few 'blanks' left on the world map are being filled: that is, ever more regions and niches are being integrated into the capitalist system, so that local and national areas of self-sufficiency are tending to disappear. Incorporation into the world market and fragmentation, globalization and territorialization, are complementary processes – or, to be more precise, they are two sides of the same process of worldwide redistribution of wealth, sovereignty, power, and freedom of action.

(2)   *Transnational corporations have an interest in 'weak states'*, that is, as Zygmunt Bauman puts it, in states which are weak yet remain states. Intentionally or not, a coordinated pressure radiates from world-market players for all states that are part of the world market (or dependent on them) to eliminate anything that might hinder, slow down or restrict the freedom of movement of capital. 'Throwing wide open the gates and abandoning any thought of autonomous economic policy is the preliminary, and meekly complied with, condition of eligibility for financial assistance from world banks and monetary funds. Weak states are precisely what the New World Order, all too often looking suspiciously like a new world *disorder*, needs to sustain and reproduce itself.'[9] This also gives rise to a conflict of interests between transnational state cooperation – the European Union experiment here being the outstanding example – and neoliberal capitalism. The EU is one of the most powerful economic areas in the world. It could have a say in drawing up the rules of world trade, and in demanding the introduction and observance of social and ecological standards.

(3)   *The social welfare states of continental Europe are caught in a downward spiral.* Whereas economic players think and act trans-

nationally and thereby manage to escape the control of national states, the consequences of transnational economics – rising unemployment and poverty – have to be dealt with by national states. On the one hand, under the growing pressure of the world market, the testing hour has arrived when social networks will have to prove whether they can be further funded and sustained; on the other hand, the moment of truth is also now approaching, since the costs explosion coincides with a fall in income tax revenue from employees and a globalization of the profits of transnational corporations.

(4) *The replacement of labour by knowledge and capital.* Global capitalism can get by on less and less human labour-power as it opens up more and more new fields for the production of profits. Human labour and the mass organizations that represent it – trade unions and workers' parties – are everywhere losing bargaining-power and social influence. At the same time, a growing number of people are excluded from the labour market and from opportunities for material and social security and integration. Consequently, not only are inequalities on the rise, but the *character* of social inequalities is dramatically changing as ever larger circles of people are excluded as in principle 'economically inactive'.

(5) *The twofold relativity of poverty.* In these mutually reinforcing processes of inclusion and exclusion, the face of poverty has also been changing: it has risen dramatically, and it has fragmented in several ways. As Zygmunt Bauman argues, the thread of social communication between (globalized) rich and (localized) poor is threatening to snap, since between the winners from globalization at the top and the losers from globalization at the bottom there are no longer any arenas in which greater equality and justice can be struggled for and enforced.

At the same time, those who are excluded – unlike the proletariat in the nineteenth and early twentieth centuries – have lost any means of potentially asserting their power, simply because they are no longer needed. All they have left is naked force to create a public outcry about their condition.

Finally, the subdivisions of poverty are again refracted in a 'double relativity'. The 'simple relativity' of poverty refers to *standards*: it means there are no absolute standards of poverty, only relative standards that apply to different regions of world society

(Africa, Asia, Europe, etc.). In the case of 'double relativity', the relativity of standards is further refracted in transcultural, transnational habitats. 'Transnational poverty' means that people live their lives within the contradiction of transnational standards of poverty. In Britain, for example, people who are considered homeless may still live well by the standards applied to their family in India or the Caribbean.[10] These fragmentations are also essential to the intensification of poverty.

(6) *Contradictions of self-organized glocal life operate as criteria of exclusion.* It is often stressed (especially by this author) that, beyond the securities of tradition and the left–right schema of political action, the second modernity offers new opportunities for freedom and personal development. But the question is: *For whom?* The contradictions of the second modernity must also be interpreted as a sharpening of the challenges to social integration which more and more people do not meet. These 'failures' of intensified competition are regarded as 'weak', 'at risk' or 'handicapped'; they are people with few or no recognized qualifications, whose health may be bad or whose strengths (for example, athletic, artistic or manual skills) count for little in the current scale of achievements. They are all in danger of going downhill and joining the circle of those permanently excluded by the rules of access.

(7) *Capitalism without work is matched by a Marxism without utopia.* The neo-Marxist picture of the capitalist world-system no longer has any utopian energy, any systematic political hope or fantasy. For its analysis cannot find any place for a political subject. In the long run, is it not inevitable that such a cosmopolitan neo-Marxism will join in the great lament at the irrevocable sinking of the *Titanic*?

World risk society: the meltdown of the iron cage of modernity

An awareness of global ecological threats drives many into fatalism. Faced with the global industrial megasystem and its machinery of self-destruction, how is it possible to act politically with a clear vision – that is, without lying to oneself? But in this naively realist misperception of 'intrinsic' dangers, there is – if I may say so

– a failure to recognize the extra something contained in the theory of world risk society.[11]

For the outstanding feature of conflicts resulting from risks is that previously depoliticized areas of decision-making now find themselves politicized by the public awareness of risks. They are opened to public doubt and debate – mostly in the face of resistance from the powerful institutions that monopolize such decisions. In world risk society, then, subjects and themes which have been handled behind closed doors – for example, economic investment decisions, the chemical composition of products and medicines, scientific research programmes, the development of new technologies – may from one day to the next be made public and spelt out in minute detail. Everything suddenly has to be publicly justified, and it becomes possible to draw up a legal and institutional framework that will legitimate and permanently establish this important extension of democracy.

An ironical way of putting this would be to say that there is discussion everywhere, by appointment, about unintended, unforeseen problems before they arise, even *before* the products and technologies at issue are actually invented. Crucially, however, this widening and deepening of democracy to the non-political spheres of economy and science (and partly also to the private sphere) has up to now been blocked by antiquated 'defining relationships', where the onus of proof falls not on those who profit from risks but on those who are affected by them.

In world society, therefore, the public perception of risks gives rise to a *self-critical* society (at least verbally open to other ways of acting and thinking), one in which, for example, insurance companies contradict true-believer technologists. The latter may say 'there's zero risk', while the former – who *in extremis* may have to answer for the 'zero risk' – say 'uninsurable', because the *economic* risk (of nuclear energy or genetic engineering, for example) is too high.[12]

At the same time, the contours are beginning to emerge of a *utopian ecological democracy*, which for me would be the essence of a *responsible* modernity. What 'responsible' means, what it includes, may be explained by reference to the 'technological citizenship' debate in Anglo-American philosophy and scientific research. Here a society is depicted which debates the consequences of technological and economic development *before* the key decisions are taken; which places the burden of proof concerning future risks and dangers upon those who might cause them, and no longer upon those potentially or actually harmed or endangered by them. There is a move away from the principle that the person responsible pays to the principle that the person responsible *proves* what (possible) harm his or her enterprise may bring into the world.

A way out of the self-perpetuating global drive for technological novelty might be found, for example, in a politically backed search for *alternative technologies* in some of the more dubious areas in question. The way in which scientists think of technological development would then have to focus on alternatives and not on the production of material constraints. Perhaps the sting could be taken out of a particular course if, at the most advanced level, there was an alternative that had the advantages of the rejected option without its disadvantages. Perhaps the global network could politically be offered something (solar energy, for example) whose ability to assert itself derived precisely from its attractiveness for the networks in question. In this case, technological policy would become a vanguard policy promoting crucial alternatives by democratic political means.

Finally, a new system of controls would have to be found or invented which, for both legal and scientific purposes, redefined the meaning of terms such as 'adequate proof', 'truth' and 'justice' in the face of dangers likely to affect everyone. This would require nothing less than a *second Enlightenment*, which would open our eyes and our institutions to the immaturity of the first industrial civilization and the dangers it posed to itself.

Where will this political mobilization come from, this (if things go well) 'compulsory democratization' under the impact of risk-conflicts? Risk society means that the past loses its power to determine the present. Instead, the future – something non-existent, constructed or fictitious – takes its place as the cause of present experience and action. When we talk about risks, we argue over something which is *not* the case, but which *might* come to pass if there is not an *immediate* change of direction. Risks in which people believe are the whip driving the present to make some move. The more threatening the shadows cast by future prospects, the more lasting are the disruptions that can be brought about today through the dramaturgy of risk.

Definitions of risk, successfully asserted, are a magic political wand through which a smugly settled society learns to fear itself and, against its will, is compelled to become politically active in its core areas. The vivid symbolic staging of risks is, in this sense, an antidote to a narrow 'carry on as before' mentality. A society that sees itself as a risk society is in a state rather like that of a (Catholic) sinner who confesses his or her sins, so as at least to philosophize about the possibility and desirability of a 'better' life in harmony with nature and the conscience of the world. For only a few want a real change of course. Most wish that nothing should happen *and* want to complain about it. Then it is possible to enjoy the bad 'good life', as well as the threats facing it.

In this subversive, unintended and unforeseen self-questioning of the bases of political life ('reflexive modernization'[13]), which is everywhere set in train by the perception of risks, something finally happens which sociologists who swear by Max Weber scarcely consider possible: namely, the institutions themselves start to move. According to Weber's diagnosis, modernity was changing into an iron cage in which people had to sacrifice themselves like the fellahin of Ancient Egypt, only now on the altars of rationality. The theory of world risk society maintains the opposite: that the cage of modernity is opening.

Anyone who allows himself to get worked up about a risk in a naively realist sort of way, fails to appreciate that what wreak such havoc are not the particular side-effects (the particular 'poison of the week') but the effects which those effects have within the institutions of society. It is not only cows but also ruling parties, officials, meat markets, consumers, and so on, who become 'mad'.

Global society without democratic politics

'The time for petty politics is over,' wrote Friedrich Nietzsche more than a hundred years ago. 'The next century will bring a struggle for domination of the earth – a *compulsion* to politics on a grand scale.'[14] What does 'world society' mean if it is conceived as a new form of politics? In this section the concept of a 'stateless' world society will be examined, and it will be explained why the term 'world society' itself obscures the fact that the reality in question is essentially nothing other than a subversive form of politics (subversive, that is, in relation to an understanding of politics based on the national state).

The distinction between a first and a second modernity, between national and world society, refers not only to different social epochs but to *different understandings of society*. It is, above all, this non-identity of the same concept 'society' which obstructs people's vision of the second modernity.

Three further concepts – state, location and functional differentiation – may be used as points of reference for a reformulation of the concept of society.

World society without a (world) state

'The sociology of globalization,' writes Martin Albrow,

> denotes the most recent attempt to find answers to questions that every generation raises. Only by asking these questions anew can each generation discover what it is. It is therefore not only economic issues, nor only technological issues, which are involved in globalization. Nor is it just a matter of the greatest challenge facing heads of corporations and governments. It is all these things, but it is also something much more important. It concerns how you and I lead our lives.[15]

And Mark Poster asks:

> When I speak to a friend in Paris directly or by e-mail, while sitting in California; when I follow political and cultural events around the world without leaving home; when data containing my personal profile are used by governments and corporations world-wide without my knowledge and without my being able to stop them; when I shop at home using my computer: Where am I then? Who am I?

Irrevocable globality, as we said before, means that we have long been living in a world society. This refers essentially to the whole set of social and power relations that are not organized on a national basis, and the experience of living and acting *across borders*. The unity of state, society and individual underpinning the first modernity is in the course of dissolution. World society does *not* mean world state society or world economy society; it means a *non-state* society, a social aggregate for which territorial state guarantees of order, as well as the rules of publicly legitimated politics, lose their binding character.

'Statelessness' means that a *competitive relationship* exists between national states and national societies, on the one hand, and the restless imprecision of the ties, players and arenas of world society, on the other hand. Whereas in the first modernity the field of international relations was dominated by the cooperation and opposition of national states and players, this is no longer the case in the second modernity. If the state in the Western tradition is conceived as a 'civil association' (Michael Oakeshott), which serves to facilitate and concentrate social, political and economic activities of its citizens, then the advent of globalization involves not only an erosion of the tasks and institutions of the state, but also a fundamental transformation of its underlying premisses. The second modernity brings into being, alongside the world society of national states, a powerful non-state world society different from previously existing forms of political legitimation, which is made up of transnational players of the most diverse kinds. These players have the following key features: (a) They act across borders, even transnationally, and thereby annul the territorial principle of the national state. (b) Their activity is in many respects more inclusive, less exclusive, than that of state players. (Thus transnational corporations and Greenpeace activists are active *in several states at once*, their players belong to different nations, and so on.) (c) They are often more effective than the authorities of national states, as measured by key criteria of the success of state action (for example, lower unemployment and security of well-being, but also the recovery of basic rights). Thus transnational corporations may create or revoke jobs and prosperity in a particular location; while Amnesty International draws public attention to human rights violations that particular states pass over in silence for diplomatic reasons. (d) Non-state transnational players create their own 'inclusive sovereignty', as it were, by playing off the exclusive territorial states against one another.

The more these various elements intertwine and reinforce one another, the more durably are the authority, control, legitimacy and moulding power of states called into question, from both within and without. In the field of action of world society, we are thus dealing with *politicization through a depoliticization of states*. 'A critical threshold may be crossed when the cumulative effect of globalization in strategically decisive issue-areas undermines the general capacity of the state to pursue the common good or the capacity of the state to be a true civil association.'[16] As the *Financial Times* reports, 53 per cent of all value-creation now derives from transnational rather than purely national corporations. Accordingly, national states and governments have less and less power to influence job creation and the prosperity of citizens.

This competitive relationship between state and transnational players also means that it is not a question of *either* national *or* world society: what exists between these two forms of society is,

rather, a subversive relationship of mutual challenge and displace-
ment. On the one hand, the world market threatens to undermine
and replace politics; on the other hand, politics is everywhere faced
with new labours of Hercules in determining the shape of world
markets.

> It is not diagnosis that is lacking. What needs to be explained is the
> cautiousness about a perspective that directs people's gaze at the
> (rocky as ever) path to a transnational internal politics. Why is it so
> outlandish to explore institutions and procedures which are neces-
> sary for the construction of common interests 'with a cosmopolitan
> intent' and for a 'regime of global welfare'?[17]

The players of world society, seen through the eyes of national
players, are in a way 'underground players' of questionable legitimacy and loyalty. But those same players of world society go
around with their noses in the air, since their opportunities for
action and power increase as they learn how to deal with national
controls and players. Often they are the *winners* of globalization,
where 'winner' may also be understood as a personified comparative in the narrow, monetary sense of 'gain'. In the global era,
*national states do not exist without world societies, and world societies
do not exist without national states and societies*. It is the resulting
blockages, breakdowns and unresolved questions which give this
situation its political charge.

If we again focus on the aspect of world society, we can see that
'stateless' here means two further things: to exaggerate a little, it
means being (still) *without order*, and (still) *without institutions*.
'World' in 'world society' denotes 'diversity without unity'
(Albrow), while 'national' society signifies 'unity with limited
diversity'.[18]

Multilocal world society

World society means 'society' that is not territorially fixed, not
integrated, not exclusive. But it does not mean that this kind of
social diversity and cultural difference knows *no local ties at all*.
Rather, the type of local tie *cancels the equation of spatial and social
distance* implicit in the national picture of society, so that 'transnational lifeworlds' come into being. These transnational phenomena
should not be thought of as being the same as 'inter-state'

phenomena. Transnational coexistence means social proximity *in spite of* geographical distance – or, social distance *in spite of* geographical proximity.

What are the consequences of this for people's identity? Certainly not (as empirical studies show) anomie, disintegration, or dissolution of the social.[19] In multilocal, transnational, 'glocal' biographies, the points at which people come into contact and affect one another are both broader and more numerous. Perhaps a good example would be the (virtual) forms of computer-assisted communication. The idea of a 'global village' is false, not least because it leads people to believe in the return of 'community'. But what is so special about the electronic media is that *in principle* they are capable of mobilizing people, and thus have a *potentially* political momentum. Electronic communication makes possible what has previously been excluded: namely, active, simultaneous and reciprocal contact between individuals across all frontiers constituted by countries, religions and continents.

We should not complain about the media as if they were some brave new world, nor underestimate the political opportunities that come with them. Everyone can take part simply by flicking a switch: they are action-oriented media geared to the moment, rather than contemplative and geared to tradition. In this way, it *might* be possible to get beyond that nightmare image of social dissolution which is held up as a foil to boost place-monogamous ways of thinking and living. Unlike community tied to place, digital forms of dialogue do not rest upon kinship, tradition, social ties or even spatial vicinity, but only upon shared interests in and on the network. 'The strengths of these future scenarios', writes A. Bühl, 'lie in their depiction of the expanded scope for individual dialogue and action. Their weaknesses lie in their postulation of a kind of classlessness – a fetishism of cyberspace which no longer sees the simple fact that the network is limited to barely 1 per cent of the world's population.'[20]

Undifferentiated world society

According to the image dominant in both sociology and society, modernity breaks down into a number of more and more independent institutional fields, or – in a different terminology – functional or existential spheres. These are separated from, and against, one another by virtue of the autonomous 'developmental logic' (N.

Luhmann speaks of 'communicative codes') that each of them obeys. This functional structuring of modern society may also be related to the individual professions and groups of experts which have each built a 'realm' of their own upon a special monopoly: law, medicine, economics, technology. Many even consider that journalists have monopolized the public media in an analogous manner. This theory of functional social differentiation often goes together with the criticism that the individual spheres have for a long time revolved around themselves, so that what was once 'functional rationality' has long become 'organized irrationality'.

Several possible correctives have been proposed to this immunization of independent spheres against one another. Many think that success will depend upon the extent to which individuals, in their concrete interactions, actually bridge the gap between the spheres. Others maintain that a kind of programmed systems-coordination might establish the points of view necessary for co-operation. Yet others are convinced that a focus upon the totality must be politically generated, and that the central task of the state policy sub-system must be to renew and expand its capacity for coordination and direction.[21]

Serious doubts have been raised about all these proposals. In recent years, however, the whole debate has taken a new turn because of the controversy about globalization. Suddenly the issue is no longer how the self-propelling course of functional differentiation with all its resulting problems can be slowed down and brought under control, but, on the contrary, whether the imaginative universe of functionally differentiated spheres, each with its own independent logic, has not become questionable in the wake of globalization.

This will become clearer if we briefly look at one dimension of globalization, the economic dimension. This really became significant when the movements of global capital not only escaped the controls of the state but no longer appeared to obey any comparable regulatory principle. The frame of reference has thus shifted as the global economy as a whole has moved into the field of vision. And since it does not recognize any regulatory power, the orthodox functionalist system has, like the national state, become open to question within world society. In the age of global capital, it becomes unclear not only what a national economy means but, more fundamentally, how 'economy' and 'economic activity' in general should be conceived in distinction to 'politics', and so on.

Much the same is true of all the other functionally differentiated spheres. What do politics, law, culture, family and civil society mean in transnational world society? As we have already seen, two concepts must be distinguished here: world society as the sum of national states and societies, and world societies of transnational actors and spaces. The former may be conceived as functionally differentiated, but not the latter. This raises the question of whether the theory of functional differentiation did not have the unity of state and society – national-state society – as its tacit historical precondition, so that with the declining significance of the national state, its ideal of a society governed by functional differentiation has also lost meaning and reality.

At the same time, the tables are now being turned. In the paradigm of a functionally differentiated first modernity, 'society' appeared as a residual category, as a residual society, so to speak, whose occasional 'highs' obstructed rather than assisted the smoothly rational course of systemic processes. Now, however, the opposite is true. 'World society' must be theorized and empirically investigated as the horizon within which capital, culture, technology and politics merrily come together to roam *beyond* the regulatory power of the national state.

'Globalization', argues M. Albrow, 'again places the understanding and organization of society right at the top of the agenda of public debate' – with a compelling force that has never been present since the age of Marxism and class confrontation. To be sure, we are now faced not with a 'class crisis' but with a 'crisis' resulting from the unfamiliar and chaotic quality of world society. The issue, according to Albrow, is one of 'identity'.[22] Who am I? Where am I? Where and to whom do I belong? These are the key questions of the second modernity.

In other words, world society refers to a kind of *new world*, a kind of undiscovered continent, which is being revealed in the transnational no-man's-land between national states and societies. Consequently, a *difference in power* is opening up between national politics and the scope for action within world society. This is especially visible in the relationship of national states to multinational corporations.[23] But it also affects such things as the implementation of transnational law, the fight against transnational crime, the elaboration of a transnational cultural policy, or the opportunities for action by transnational social movements.

Prospects for a transnational state

Many writers see the global age as spelling the end of the national state and therefore of democracy. 'The end of the nation brings with it the death of politics,' writes Jean-Marie Guéhenno.

> Once solidarity and common interests no longer have any natural place, there is a breakdown in the harmonious order of a society where the various authorities lock together as in a pyramid. There are no longer any major decisions from which minor ones can be derived; no longer any laws from which rules and regulations can be drawn. Just as the local community is no longer 'contained' in the region or the region in the national state, a minor decision can no longer be derived from a major one. It is thus at the level of decision-making that the spatially defined concept of power moves from crisis to defeat. Decisions are no longer taken in a linear mode in which each entity has a clear-cut competence. Instead they break up into fragments, and the traditional political debate over fundamental principles and ideas, over ideology and the social order, fades away, or rather, comes apart at the seams. It thus mirrors the splitting and professionalization of the decision-making process itself. In the United States, which is at the forefront of the institutional reconstruction of power, one can most clearly see how the logic of existing institutions is becoming exhausted and politics itself pulled into the process of decomposition.[24]

Doubtless this French neo-Spenglerism of the global age also reflects an unrecognized mental block. There is neither capacity nor desire to imagine any alternative to the national architecture of politics and democracy. Against this mental virus nothing is as important as persistent (three times a day!) enquiry into the possibility of alternatives. Here I should like to suggest the alternative of the transnational state as at least one possible response to globalization. Underlying this is the consideration that the (national) state is not only antiquated but also indispensable – both to guarantee internal and geopolitics, basic political rights, etc.,[25] and to give political shape and transnational regulation to the process of globalization. Transnational states are thus *strong* states, whose power to shape politics develops out of cooperative answers to globalization. This is why they may be treated as 'realistic utopias' (A. Giddens) of a *third way*. Against the mental block of the national political monopoly, and against the nightmare vision of an imperial world state whose claim on power could never be escaped, this reformulation and reformation of international political space is intended to facilitate a complex architecture of sovereignty and identity. There is one crucial prerequisite if it is to come true: the various national states must be joined together through the cooperative procedures of a binding cosmopolitan community of states,

> *in such a way that this is visible in each country's internal politics.* The decisive question, then, is whether a *consciousness* of compulsory cosmopolitan solidarity can emerge in the civil societies and public political arenas of regimes that are to a large extent growing together. Only under this pressure of an effective change in citizens' consciousness can the players capable of global action come to think of themselves as members of a community whose only option is cooperation and respect for one another's interests.[26]

Such a change of perspective – from international relations to a transnational internal policy – is not to be expected from the ruling elites unless public attention is in each case directed over the national garden fences, unless a crucial interest of the various sections of the population also speaks in favour of it. In other words, transnational states will become possible only through *conscious realization* of the necessity of transnational states.[27]

The model of the transnational state is a hybrid in which a number of basic features that may often be regarded as mutually exclusive are ideo-typically recombined and fused together. First of all, then, transnational states are *non-national states*, and hence also *non-territorial states* (at least in any narrow sense). They should be thought of as a complete refutation or countermodel to the container theory of state and society.

Second, the model of the transnational state negates the *national* state but also affirms (the concept of) *the state*. The understanding of the state is freed from the trap of nationally centred theory. At the same time, it opens out towards a concept of the state which (a) recognizes globality in its many dimensions as a basic and irreversible fact, and (b) considers the determination and organization of the transnational to be crucial for a redefinition and revitalization of politics (in the sense not only of the state but also of civil society).

Third, however, transnational states are *not international* or *supranational* states (in the sense of regional world states). For models built around the concepts of international organization, multilateralism or multi-level politics within a supranational system, the national state is still the point of reference, whether as opposite number (international organization), as elementary unit to be outgrown through general norms or specified reciprocity between member-states (multilateralism), or as self-standing supranational state (multi-level politics). Transnational states, too, as multilateralism and embryonic multi-level politics emphasize, are to be understood as a model of cooperation among states – and to this extent they are liable to many of the 'traps of political integration' identified by Fritz W. Scharpf. But the central difference is that within the theory of transnational states (where plurality is also necessary), the system of political coordinates no longer results from national separateness and antagonism, but runs along the globalization–localization axis.

Fourth, transnational states are *glocal* states, which, in accordance with the principle of inclusive distinction, see themselves as provinces of world society and acquire from this their position in the world market and within polycentric world politics.

The model of the transnational state differs from other models of cooperation among states by making *globality the irrevocable foundation of political thought and action*. With my experimental model of the transnational state, political theory and actual politics open themselves up to the global age: they bid farewell to the illusory necessities of a political epoch that declared the national state to be the *non plus ultra* or the necessary evil. Of course, what is put forward here should not be taken as more than a beginning that raises more questions than it answers. It rests upon two fundamental propositions.

First, there is no point at all in trying to resist globalization by hiding oneself away, or even by making oneself as mobile as possible. Besides, such a protectionist response would mean deafening and blinding oneself to the new directions that become *possible* as things break down. This historical opportunity, which can very easily be missed (or messed up), arises from the fact that, within the nexus of world society, the violent trauma of nation-state modernity can be, if not overcome, then at least alleviated and narrowed down. We stand at a threshold where not only catastrophes *but also* cosmopolitan society are possible. To overlook this 'also-possibility' by focusing only upon the catastrophes is an unrealistic attitude. I would expressly add, however, that *unwaver-*

ing scepticism in response to overhasty optimism about the pacification of world society is the necessary precondition for this 'also-possibility' to be seized.

How do forms of society 'with a cosmopolitan intent' become possible? The second basic proposition states that they become possible through transnational cooperation and relations of dependence within the economic, political, military, legal, cultural and other dimensions. In the first modernity, there were only two paths to stability within a world of national players: either equilibrium (balance of terror) or hegemony. In the age of globalization, by contrast, the alternative is loss of national sovereignty or transnational cooperation.

In summarizing what has been argued so far, we should here examine certain aspects of the two axioms.

Recognition of world society and its dynamic   For the paradigm of the national state, the chapters of this book which demonstrate the transnational dynamic of capital, labour, culture and society amount to little short of a declaration of war. Admittedly there is no actual enemy, but the foundations are removed from a politics based upon the national state – and in a way that appears to be even worse, since globalization is often viewed almost as a virtual declaration of war ('imperialism', 'Americanization') and responded to with protectionism. In the transnational understanding of politics, as we have seen, globalization is conceived as a form of politicization: that is, the degree of successful integration of world society is made the basis for a reorientation and reorganization of political space. This first involves the abandonment of two principles of the doctrine of the national state: the *equation* of state and society, and the *exclusive territorial association* of state and society (for example, through overlapping membership).

Transnational cooperation   There is no answer to globalization at the level of the national state. Such one-country politics is becoming ever falser – which is to say, more cost-intensive (where 'costs' are not to be understood only in an economic sense). Going-it-alone *destroys* state politics, whereas transnational cooperation *gives it fresh life.*

From *national–national* to *global–local*, the framework has been changing. What forms the core of politics is not confrontation between exclusive claims to sovereignty and national identity, but rather location within the nexus of world society, of economic, ecological, cultural and civic globality and globalization. The key concepts of politics and society must be reformulated accordingly.

Provinces of world society   Exclusive opposition along national lines is being supplanted by inclusive opposition as niches, locations or 'provinces' of world society. 'Inclusive opposition' means recognition of world society as the common framework, and particular location within it through the stressing, staging and animation of regional specificities. As regards the dimension of labour, this could mean trying to strengthen world-market location not by doing and producing the same as what everyone else does and produces – for example, the 'market miracle-weapons' of genetic engineering and microelectronics – but by exploiting regional-cultural specificities to develop products and forms of labour which can establish themselves without competition.

Clearly defined diversity   Transnational also means transcultural. Assuming that transnational states recognize the non-identity of state and world society, what does this imply for cultural self-understanding? If world society means *multiplicity without unity* and national society means *unity with limited diversity*, then transnational state means *clearly defined multiplicity*. Thus, beyond either globalization or localization, variants of *glocal* cultures become capable of being experienced and recognized within the nexus of world society. In this way, the global–local axis is also expanded into a local–local axis.

Centralization and decentralization   Transnational states must be thought of in the simultaneity of centralization and decentralization. Not only is there a recognition of the diversity of transnational players; they are also accepted as having political responsibility. Hence the development of transnational link-ups is accompanied by the delegation of power and responsibility to on-site transnational civil society. But these forms of decentralization of power and responsibility are directly opposed by forms of centralization. For example, concentration of the power to issue general guidelines for social and ecological regulation of the market must always be developed, won and conquered transnationally (at least at a European level).

Opposite numbers for transnational corporations   National states suffer from a sickness unto death – falling tax revenue. Transnational states must therefore plug the tax loopholes if they are to develop power and competence in politics and social policy. After the launch of the euro, for instance, a European transnational state could largely check the speculative flow of currency by means of a minimal tax (the so-called Tobin Tax). A point of departure for the introduction of such a tax might be the fact that *international corporations too* – not only national states – *are caught up in contradictions*. On the one hand, they want to throw off the reins of the state and therefore try to keep its scope to a minimum. On the other hand, in face of the crisis dynamic in the world market, they must be able to rely upon a transnational space with predictable coordinates. For boundless poverty dissolves not only democracy but in the end also markets and profits.

Inclusive sovereignty The debate concerning national state, multi-lateralism or supranationalism always comes down to whether national states should surrender their sovereignty (their right to make laws independently) and their autonomy (power to decide over the use of force), so that higher authorities can develop a corresponding concentration of power. The division of sovereignty is thus conceived and operated as a zero-sum game, where something must be given up which will empower a supranational institution. The transnational state, by contrast, should be thought of as an *all win* game. Cooperation brings about an increase in sovereignty that works in favour both of a transnational concentration of power *and* of the local states bonded together within it.

A new medievalism Ironically, in the politics of the second modernity, formations assert themselves which bear some *medieval* characteristics. Transnational states share the loyalty of their citizens both with other regional and world authorities, and with sub-state, sub-national authorities. This 'new medievalism' (H. Bull) means that social and political ties and identities must be understood as overlapping, in terms of global, regional, national and local references and concepts of action.[28]

The global puzzle thus permits (at least) two readings. In the first, neoliberal globalism dissolves the structure of institutions of the first modernity. In the second, the reverse side of neoliberal ruthlessness – of the 'betrayal of the fatherland' by transnational economics and (sub)politics – is the establishment of transnational ways of thinking, acting and living. World-market politics, often against the intentions of those involved, compels the formation of transnational society and of transnational social ties – at least insofar as state policy understands and learns to use globalization as a new lease of life.

PART II
Perspectives

4
Errors of Globalism

In the paradigm of the first age of modernity, globalization is interpreted within the territorial compass of state and politics, society and culture. This involves an additive, not substitutive, conception of globalization, as indicated for example by 'interconnectedness'. In the paradigm of the second age of modernity, globalization changes not only the relations between and beyond national states and societies, but also the inner quality of the social and the political itself, which is indicated by a more or less 'reflexive cosmopolitization' as an institutionalized learning process – and its enemies.[1] This means globality is irreversible. We now live in a multidimensional, polycentric, contingent, political world society, in which transnational and national actors play cat and mouse with each other. Globality therefore also means: *no world state* – or, to be more precise, world society *without a world state* and *without world government*. A globally *dis*organized capitalism is the result,[2] since there is no hegemonic power and no international regime, either economic or political.

This complexity of globality should be clearly distinguished from the *new simplicity of globalism*, understood as all-penetrating, all-changing rule by the world market. It is not a question of demonizing (world) economic activity. Rather, the primacy and diktat of the world market, as promulgated in the neoliberal ideology of globalism, has to be exposed in every dimension of society for what it actually is: an antiquated economism projected on a gigantic scale, a revival of the metaphysics of history, a social revolution from above passing itself off as non-political. It is the glint in the eyes of the neoliberal 'world improvers' which can really give one a fright.[3] Let us now look in turn at the ten basic errors of globalism.

1 Metaphysics of the world market
2 So-called free world trade
3 Economic internationalization, not globalization
4 The staging of risk
5 Absence of politics as a revolution
6 The linearity myth
7 Critique of catastrophist thinking
8 Conservative protectionism
9 Green protectionism
10 Red protectionism

These ten pitfalls of globalism will then be compared with ten responses to globalization.

Metaphysics of the world market

Globalism reduces the new complexity of globality and globalization to a single (economic) dimension, which is itself *conceived in linear fashion* as a constant expansion of dependence on the world market. All other dimensions (ecological globalization, cultural globalization, political polycentrism, the emergence of transnational spaces and identities) are treated, if at all, only within the assumption of the dominance of economic globalization. World society is thus truncated and falsified as world-*market* society. In this sense, neoliberal globalism is a form of *one-dimensional* thinking and acting, a *monocausal*, economistic view of the world. Both the attraction and the danger of this by no means novel historical metaphysic of the world market have their origin in a compulsive quest for simplicity to provide some bearings in an opaque and unfathomable world.

How blind this world market metaphysics can make one is apparent from the debate on pension reform. In Germany – much as this will astonish Britons or Americans – state pensions are still, for all the bureaucracy and criticisms, an example of solidarity in practice. When neoliberal economists and politicians now argue that this is economically irrational because the same money can be much more profitably invested in private pension funds, they show once again that they understand as much about political and cultural meaning as a deaf person does about music. For not only do state pensions also protect non-contributors such as wives and children; they require a contribution from employers as well as employees (which is the concrete token of solidarity).

Pensions are thus an element of anti-capitalism at the heart of German capitalism – the non-market element, originally decreed by Bismarck, which first made capitalism feasible and then placed democracy on a stable footing after the Second World War.

What is so perfidious in the talk of state pensions as 'a system of collective compulsion' (Wolfgang Schäuble) is that an element of social solidarity is defamed and sacrificed precisely by those whose handkerchiefs are not large enough for the tears they shed in public over the loss of community.

So-called free world trade

Globalism sings the praises of worldwide free trade. A globalized economy, it is said, is best suited to raise living standards throughout the world and to eradicate social evils; even protection of the environment can be assisted through free trade, since competitive pressures force actors to be sparing with resources and encourage a healthy relationship with nature.

What this argument studiously avoids is the fact that we live in a world far removed from any Ricardian model of free trade based upon comparative cost advantage. High unemployment in the so-called Third World and post-Communist Europe forces the governments there to pursue an export-oriented economic policy, at the price of poor social and environmental standards. With low wages, often pitiful working conditions and 'no-union' zones, these countries compete for foreign capital both with one another and with rich Western countries.

Especially cynical is the assertion that world trade is ultimately to everyone's benefit because it sharpens competition and reduces costs. For in reality, there are two ways of reducing costs: either by raising the level of technology, organization, and so on, or by violating labour and production norms fit for human beings. A firm can also prosper through such violations, but only by falling into a late variant of transnational piracy.

Economic internationalization, not globalization

Globalism does not only confuse multidimensional glocalization with one-dimensional economic globalization; it also confuses economic globalization with internationalization of the economy. The evidence is supposed to show that, strictly speaking, one cannot (yet?) talk of globalization in the regions of the world economy, *but only of internationalization*. There is a clear strengthening of *trans*national trade and production relations *within* and *between* certain parts of the world – America, Asia and Europe. The proof of this is that trade and foreign investment still mostly take place among these three great economic blocs, so that there is sometimes talk of a triadization of the world economy. For Germany this means *inter alia* that, even today, low-wage competition from Asian countries or the former Eastern bloc is statistically negligible (around 10 per cent).

> As a result of the globalization of markets and the internationalization of production, it is mainly the labour-intensive branches and low-skilled labour which have come under pressure from competition in the world economy. Concretely, this means that demand has been falling for low-skilled labour because of relocation of production abroad; this takes the form of wage adjustments and direct investments, as well as a rise in imports. Long-term changes in the internal economy, which are leading to the progressive replacement of labour with capital and knowledge, are reinforced by developments in the world economy. In the future, no doubt, competitive pressure will also become more intense upon capital-intensive and knowledge-intensive branches of production, as well as upon more highly skilled sections of the labour force, because economic advances by rising nations and by countries in Central and Eastern Europe will make them appear in certain branches of production as additional competitors alongside the old industrialized countries. It is currently uncertain how the demand for skilled labour will evolve in Germany against a background of global markets and international production.[4]

Nevertheless, it is remarkable that Germany's foreign trade is still mostly conducted with the industrialized countries of the West.

> Germany carries out its external trade overwhelmingly with the Western industrialized countries. In 1993, 77.29 per cent of its exports and 77.81 per cent of its imports came from this region. Within this group of countries, the bulk of direct investment was carried out with EU countries. *A strong Eurocentredness of German external trade* may be noted. This is due to the geographical proximity of these countries, and also, quite crucially, to the single-market effect of the EU, which discriminates against suppliers from countries outside the region. Apart from the EU, the largest trading

partner from the industrialized West is the USA, which in 1993 accounted for 7.01 per cent of Germany's imports and 7.27 per cent of its exports.

In 1993, roughly 20 per cent of German external trade was conducted with the typical low-wage countries of Africa, America and Asia, as well as with the reforming countries and state-trading countries of Asia. In 1993 Germany received 22.14 per cent of its imports from this group of countries. In the other direction, 22.44 of its exports went there. The structure of foreign trade shows that the German economy, supported by the single-market effect of the EU, supported itself precisely on one of the markets with the least potential for growth, whereas exports to the potentially growing markets of South-East Asia and South America performed rather modestly. [...]

For the future, it can be expected that import pressure will also increase on capital-intensive and knowledge-intensive goods. In particular, the fast-developing nations and the countries of Central and Eastern Europe will appear as competitors in this field. This will be especially true of 'mobile Schumpeter industries', where research and production can be easily separated from each other. These include the chemical industry, the rubber goods industry, the office equipment industry, data-processing and electrical engineering. Whereas research will take place here in the industrialized countries, production (especially if it can be easily standardized) will be carried out in the fast-developing nations.[5]

The staging of risk

In the dimension of economic globalization – unlike all other dimensions – the trump card of novelty may not actually stand up to historically informed scrutiny.[6] Max Weber, for example, already in 1894 in his text on Argentinian colonial economies, dealt with questions that are stirring us today as if they were completely new.

> In its ultimate consequences, the world economy of the doctrine of free trade is a utopia without a world state and full equality in the cultural level of mankind. The road to it is a long road. So long as we are still only at the start of such a development, we shall also be acting in the interests of further development if we do not overhastily fell and cut to the size of future construction those old trunks (the historically given national economic units) from which future generations may be able to build up the economic and cultural community

of mankind, and if instead we preserve and promote them in their natural growth. – It is to a nation's advantage to eat cheap bread, but not if this happens at the expense of future generations.[7]

The counter-demand – to make the market king of social relations – is also anything but new, and even the critique of it is as old as the hills. Repetitions of repetitions, wherever one looks.[8]

Globalism, then, draws only a small part of its strength from what is at present the case. Its potential force comes more from *the staging of threats*. This is the realm of the 'might', the 'should' and the 'if ... then'.

It is thus from a variant of *risk* society that the transnational corporations derive their power. It is not 'actual damage' from *economic* globalization (for example, the transfer of jobs to low-wage countries), but the threat of the same in public discourse, which stirs up fears, intimidates people, and perhaps ultimately compels political and trade-union players to stave off the worst by themselves undertaking what investors want to see done before they are willing to invest. The *semantic hegemony* of globalism, its publicly fomented ideology, is a source of power from which the corporate sector draws its strategic potential.

Absence of politics as revolution

Globalism is a thought-virus which has by now stricken all parties, all editorial departments, all institutions. Its main article of faith is not that people must engage in economic behaviour, but that every-one and everything – politics, science, culture – should be subordi-nated to the primacy of the economic. In a way, neoliberal globalism thus resembles its arch-enemy: Marxism. It is the rebirth of Marxism as a management ideology – a kind of economic New Ageism, a revivalist movement whose apostles and prophets, instead of hand-ing out leaflets at underground stations, preach the salvation of the world in the spirit of the marketplace.

Neoliberalism is *high politics* which presents itself as completely *non*-political: the absence of politics as a revolution! Its ideology is that people do not act but fulfil world-market laws – laws which, regrettably, force them to whittle the (social) state and democracy down to a minimum.

But anyone is mistaken who thinks that globalization means the execution of world-market *laws*, which must be implemented in this and no other way. Economic globalization is *not* an automatic, mechanical process; it is a thoroughly *political project* involving transnational players, institutions and discourse-coalitions (World Bank, WTO, OECD, multinationals, other international organizations) which pursue a neoliberal economic policy.

The question, then, is who the *players* of neoliberal globalism are. And what are the *political* alternatives? How and by whom are international treaties and organizations (within the WTO, for example), the whole order of world competition, given or not given shape? Do they have room for minimum social and ecological standards to make labour and production worthy of human beings? As idle chatter or as real incentives? What influence does politics have in this, nationally and at the level of the EU? What course does the EU's external economic policy pursue? What are its development and agriculture policies? Who are the *losers* of globalization? How will the future labour-market model look within and between the countries of the EU? How should competition with neighbouring countries to the south and east, as well as between the various regions and countries of Europe, be regulated? Who will invest where? How will capital flows take place? What influence could and should national or transnational politics have on all these processes? How can the nightmarish spectre of globalism be *replaced by politics*?[9]

Even now, the growing group of losers from globalization slip through the net of political perception. No party in the USA or Europe has grasped how big a role private economic insecurity, for example, plays in the lives of employees; a gigantic hole has arisen in the centre of the political spectrum. The actual or potential losers from globalization in the middle to upper reaches of the occupational hierarchy no longer compete for better jobs and higher income to underpin their relatively modest standard of living. They think of themselves as abandoned and betrayed, both by 'right-wing' politicians in the pocket of globalization and its winners, and by 'left-wing' programmes. For, as Edward Luttwak argues, people who fear for their economic future do not need political parties 'which want to tax insecure incomes higher in order to help those who do not work'.

The linearity myth

A return-to-the-past scenario, we are told,

holds out the grim prospect of a retribalization of large swathes of humankind by war and bloodshed: a threatened balkanization of nation-states in which culture is pitted against culture, people against people, tribe against tribe, a Jihad in the name of a hundred narrowly conceived faiths against every kind of interdependence, every kind of artificial social co-operation and mutuality; against technology, against pop culture, and against integrated markets; against modernity itself as well as the future in which modernity issues. [... Another scenario] paints that future in shimmering pastels, a busy portrait of onrushing economic, technological, and ecological forces that demand integration and uniformity and that mesmerize peoples everywhere with fast music, fast computers, and fast food – MTV, Macintosh, and McDonald's – pressing nations into one homogeneous global theme park, one McWorld tied together by communications, information, entertainment, and commerce. Caught between Babel and Disneyland, the planet is falling precipitously apart and coming reluctantly together at the very same time.[10]

Seldom has a thought stereotype been as thoroughly refuted as this linearity myth.[11] For globalization has also led everywhere to a *new meaning of the local*. The expression 'global culture' is in any case misleading. What are emerging are transnational, translocal cultures or social spaces and 'landscapes':

- the tourism boom;
- small transnational worlds of experts with hardly any ties to a particular place;
- a growing number of international institutions, agencies, groups and movements, which intervene in every possible business and many impossible ones too;
- a small number of accepted languages (English, Spanish).

In the face of the arguments and research evidence given above, it can only be a sign of ignorance to be taken in by the linearity myth and to maintain that cultural convergence is a direct result of growing economic uniformity.

Critique of catastrophist thinking

Most people think that if – as Hannah Arendt nicely put it in the sixties – gainful employment is disappearing from a society based on gain, this spells a 'crisis' or even a 'catastrophe'. But what may appear thus to natives of the work society is, from a historical bird's-eye view, also a fantastic vision. Many generations and epochs have dreamt of finally throwing off or loosening the yoke of work, as more and more wealth is generated with less and less human labour-power. Now the time has come, but no one wants anything to do with it.

Methodologically, this means that in the transition from the first to the second modernity we are dealing with a fundamental transformation, a paradigm shift, a departure into the unknown world of globality, but not with a 'catastrophe' or 'crisis', if the concept of crisis means that we could return to the status quo ante by taking the 'right' (= usual) measures.

The mass unemployment shaking Europe is also no 'crisis', since a return to full employment is an illusory goal. But nor is it a 'catastrophe', since the replacement of labour with partly or fully automated production could, if properly applied, bring epochal opportunities for an expansion of human freedom. These opportunities must certainly be spelt out and politically grasped in opposition to the old thinking, and for this we need a *public brainstorming*, an application of political-institutional fantasy. This is the only way of raising and answering the question: How is democracy possible beyond the fiction of a society with full employment?[12]

Neoliberal globalism not only spreads fear and terror; it also paralyses politically. If nothing can be done, then the only response in the end is to take cover, to hide oneself away under the bristles. Infected with the thought-virus of globalism, all parties are giving ground to arguments and ideologies based upon a protectionist reaction. Apparently opposed to globalism but actually under its spell, a huge 'black'–red–green coalition of protectionism is taking shape, which with different ends in mind defends the old order (of battle) against the rushing realities and adversities of the second modernity.[13]

Conservative protectionism

Conservative protectionists are caught up in a special contradiction. They idolize the nation-state yet dismantle it with a neoliberal crusade in favour of a free world market.

Conservative protectionism, however, is not only a contradiction *in flagrante* between thought and deed, a posture which with one hand swears on the values of the nation (family, religion, community, etc.) and with the other displays missionary zeal in fuelling a neoliberal dynamic that undermines and dissolves those same conservative values. Those who keep rolling back the social state accept that the foundation of 'social civil rights' (T. M. Marshall) and therefore political freedom is full of holes.

In the end, the neoliberal strategy of globalism is self-contradictory. It fails just when it is universalized (in thought).

> The attempt to win jobs by improving one's own relative productivity is, of course, to some extent legitimate. In a country such as the German Federal Republic, however, where there continue to be export surpluses of industrial goods, this is from a certain point of view an extremely questionable undertaking. Full employment here depends upon the willingness of other countries to accept still higher trade deficits with Germany. So there are political limits to the strategy, and anyway it operates in thin air because further surplus-determined revaluations of one's own currency hit the problem sectors especially hard. Things become completely crazy, though, when the struggle for the highest productivity among the most developed industrial countries is mainly conducted through the lowering of (secondary) wage costs. This senseless competition may lead to a reduction in overall demand on markets with potentially the largest purchasing-power. The cake to be divided up then becomes smaller, while the share in the cake remains the same.[14]

Conservative protectionism is thus contradictory in two senses. It dissolves the community by which it swears, and it is economically counterproductive.

Green protectionism

Green protectionists are discovering the national state as a political biotope threatened with extinction, which defends environmental standards from world-market attack and is thus as deserving of protection as nature itself.

> An eco-protectionist politics, which would like to sever the ties between markets with strict environmental regulations and markets with less strict environmental regulations, may prove to be counterproductive. It protects industries whose environmental standards are relatively independent of those in less developed economies,

and it obstructs the spread of higher standards into regions with an inadequate environmental awareness (regions where they are in many respects the most ecologically urgent). Furthermore, the economic costs would be catastrophically high if such a detachment policy were to become universal. They would give rise to economic crises on a scale that would make any ecological policy impossible for some considerable time.

Let us avoid any misunderstanding. From an ecological point of view, many of the current transnational production chains are without question a catastrophe. North Sea crabs – which are shelled on board ships bound for Morocco, then packed in Poland before reaching the market in Hamburg – are an expression of ecological over-exploitation. But this cannot and should not be countered with protectionist measures. Instead there should be an appropriate energy tax, which reflects the real costs of transport. Since the most important ecological problems have become global, there would be no hope of overcoming such problems in a world that was altogether fragmented socially and politically. Even as things are, the situation is certainly serious enough to give grounds for scepticism. But without the processes of world economic and political integration, which on the whole are spreading and intensifying environmental regulation, the situation would look even worse than it does.[15]

In other words, green protectionism conflicts with the globality of the ecological crisis, and removes the political lever of thinking locally and acting globally.

Greens, it has to be said, are *the* intellectual-political winners of globalization: ecological questions *must* be addressed and answered as global issues. And yet, with their light-minded anti-modernism, their preference for things provincial, and their fear of losing the bureaucratic political leverage of the national state, many Green politicians are putting a spoke in their own wheel.

Red protectionism

Red protectionists dust down for every occasion the costumes of class struggle; 'globalization' is another word for 'told you so'. It is a Marxist Easter festival of 'resurrection'. Yet what it is really about is being proved right on a basis of utopian blindness.

In the age of globalization, there can be no doubt that a politics of social reconciliation and social conscience ends up in a most uncomfortable dilemma. Without a reduction in social costs and (secondary) wage costs, the numbers of unemployed will increase; without new jobs, however, the whole system of social protection built upon paid employment threatens to collapse. If the volume of gainful employment measured in working hours per employee now contracts – not (or not only) because of opportunities to export jobs to the new and menacing-sounding 'tiger states' now so close in the erstwhile 'Far East', but above all because of productivity leaps in the labour that has remained behind[16] – then a social policy that banks on paid employment will, to put it mildly, find itself having to rack its brains to come up with a solution.

Many therefore turn to the radical option of rejecting the whole alternative that has led to this unfortunate dilemma: world trade (for which read: capitalism) plus the social welfare state. This is seen as a compromise terminated by globalization, and now to be thrown upon the rubbish heap of history.[17]

A milder variant, involving left *nostalgia for the social state*, fails to recognize that the crisis of the social system is not conjunctural. An epoch is drawing to a close – the century which began with Bismarck's social legislation already in place, and which in its final third seemed to a whole generation to have really solved, on the basis of participation in gainful employment, the great task of assuring a life of freedom and security for the majority of people. This solution to the 'social question' is now in turn becoming the social problem. And this means in general that anyone who wants to change something *has to be 'unjust'*, to reduce or disallow entitlements, to encourage and protect people's own initiatives, and thus doggedly to promote a different logic, a different morality of social policy.

A reform of *income support* in Germany, for example, has become indispensable because the old system is proving less and less suitable for protection against the mass risks of long-term unemployment. A needs-oriented minimum insurance, including the provision of basic cover against mass risks by local authorities and regional and federal government, would be a fair and important reform measure. There are already models, even ones which would help to reduce costs without increasing poverty. However, such strategies for a 'reflexive modernization' of income support have so far, like so much else, foundered on the structural conservatism in all parties and the lack of a will for reform among politicians and in society at large.

5

Responses to Globalization

There can be only one conclusion: the debate must begin on how responsible globalization can be *politically* moulded and achieved.

First of all, this presupposes the kind of radical critique we have already made of *the neoliberal ideology of globalism*, of its economic one-dimensionalism, its one-way-street linear thinking, its world-market authoritarianism which poses as non-political yet acts in a highly political way. It is thus clear that globality and globalization are neither an illusion blown up and publicly staged so that capitalism can shake off the fetters of the social state; nor concepts to enforce general obsequiousness by referring to new natural laws of the world market. It cannot be repeated often enough that the age of globality brings not the end of politics but a new beginning.

If the globalization shock that marks the transition to a second modernity is ultimately political, this is because *all* actors and organizations at *all* levels of society *must* confront both the paradoxes and the challenges of the structurally revolutionary dynamic of globalization. Interestingly enough, this 'must' blows apart the old Left–Right schema. There is a left-wing and a right-wing nostalgia: the former exalts the social state, the latter the national state. Both agree in defending the national status quo against the 'invasion of the world market'.

But what political responses to globality can we see beginning to emerge?

Having briefly considered the ten errors of globalist thinking, let us now confront them with ten responses to globality and globalization.

1 International cooperation
2 Transnational state or 'inclusive sovereignty'
3 Joint ownership of capital
4 Reorientation of educational policy
5 Are transnational corporations undemocratic or anti-democratic?
6 An alliance for civil labour
7 What comes after the Volkswagen export nation? New cultural, political and economic goals
8 Experimental cultures, niche markets and the self-renewal of society
9 Public entrepreneurs, people working for themselves
10 A social contract against exclusion?

International cooperation

A first political response to globalization – one especially favoured by social democratic modernizers – is collaboration among national states to limit or obstruct the 'horse-trading' whereby global firms minimize their tax obligations and maximize state subsidies.

Here the task of politics is seen as explaining to the public that globalization cannot mean the abandonment of everything to market forces. With globalization there is a growing need for binding international regulation, for international conventions and institutions that cover cross-border transactions. In this respect, globalization must go hand in hand with better policy coordination among sovereign national states, better international supervision of banks and financial institutions, an end to fiscal dumping between states (within the European Union, for example), closer cooperation within international organizations, and strengthening of those organizations to ensure greater flexibility and efficiency.

As is the case at national level, it must also hold for international economic relations that the market needs a political regulatory framework.

The social and ecological market economy is the political system of coordinates of the European Union. We would argue that this model of a market economy with social and ecological responsibility should now also become the social basis for a new world economic order. This could create the best conditions for firms to compete over performance and ideas, and for fair trade to benefit everyone concerned.

For this we need international agreements within a framework of supranational institutions. Such institutions already exist: the European Union, G-7, the OECD, the International Monetary Fund, and the new World Trade Organization. The economic preconditions are also present. For the international trade and investment flows that make up the core of globalization are mainly concentrated within the so-called triad (the European economies plus the non-European industrial economies of G-7, the USA, Canada and Japan). So-called globalization does not lie outside our political sphere of influence. We must use the political scope for action to achieve better international cooperation. Then it will be possible to master the present problems of globalization, as well as those likely to arise in the future.[1]

Such an approach looks for answers to globality not within a supranational mega-state or even world state, but in a closing of ranks among national states. These are supposed to concert their efforts in such a way that: (a) they keep transnational firms within their limits and no longer allow them to play countries off against one another; (b) they can renew their political claim to power and influence. The hope is that the national age of social democracy can be revived and modernized through an international age of cosmopolitan social democracy.

There won't be an end to politics, but we do need to pioneer forms of government different from those of the classical nation-state. Special-interest groups and non-governmental organizations, now proliferating on the global scene, can't themselves provide mechanisms of government, because part of the very point of government is to resolve the different claims made by special-interest groups. There are real possibilities in David Held's model of 'cosmopolitan democracy', where he envisages association going right the way through from local government to reformed global institutions.[2]

In the second age of modernity the relationship between state, business and a society of citizens must be redefined. In the state-fixated perspective, where society is defined in national terms, it seems particularly difficult to recognize and explore the benefits of a society-of-citizens scenario for the transnational revival and encouragement of politics and democracy. One thing, however, is certain. Without stronger citizen elements, solidarity with people in other countries and a corresponding extension and restructuring of national institutions (trade unions, consumer movements) will be impossible. Trade unions, for instance, instead of being tied to plants and industries in a national framework, will have to adapt to fragile, risky labour conditions and operate along global chains of value creation.

This raises a number of key questions. What will be the material basis for transnational 'community ties' that are no longer supported by place (neighbourhood), origin (family) or nation (state-organized solidarity of citizens)? From where will they derive a sense of obligation? How will decisions be made that are at once post-national and collectively binding? Or, in other words, how is political activity possible in the global age.[3]

Transnational state or 'inclusive sovereignty'

'Economically speaking, there is much that is not new and much that is false in the current theses on globalization,' writes M. Jänicke.

> It may nevertheless be true that environmental policy is caught in the 'global trap', that environmental protection is simply too expensive in a context of global competition. This is a popular idea, of course. Even environmental activists sometimes bow to it in resignation.
>
> All the same, it is worth looking at the economics of countries that do quite a lot to protect the environment. And lo and behold, the ones with the most advanced global environmental policy are doing better economically than others! The innovators in the early seventies were the United States and Sweden. Then Japan. Then until 1994 even the Federal Republic. Today countries such as the Netherlands, Denmark and again Sweden play a leading role. Outside Europe this is also true of South Korea, among others. Interestingly enough, today's ecological vanguard is made up almost exclusively of smaller countries strongly integrated into the world market.
>
> Truly sensational, however, is the fact that even in labour-market terms they are among the more successful countries. This will become clear from a few examples. The Netherlands and Denmark, but also environmentally active New Zealand, have reduced their jobless totals by roughly a third since the recession of 1993. In Sweden, too, unemployment is declining – as it is in Scandinavia as a whole. The Nordic countries have introduced and recently even

increased various eco-taxes, including one on carbon dioxide emissions. In Denmark and Sweden, a real ecological tax reform took place during the economic crisis of 1993. Environmental protection, then, does not prevent countries from holding up in the global competition. Indeed, a reasonable environmental policy is becoming a key indicator of a country's competitiveness – according to Harvard economist Michael Porter, the prominent theorist of innovations.

Doubtless, the individual national state has not been strengthened as a result of the development of the world market. But nowadays states often act together collectively. Global networks of ministerial officials set their stamp on national environmental policy, just as do national or international environmental associations.[4]

But the decisive question is what collective interstate action means. As we have seen, the models discussed in the literature – international organization, multilateralism, multi-level politics – take the national state as their point of reference. In our alternative model of the transnational state, which cuts right across these distinctions, the shifting relationship between mutually exclusive national states and societies is replaced by a framework in which interstate alliances arise within world society and renew their specificity and independence as 'glocal states'.

The model of the transnational state thus conflicts with all other models of cooperation. Transnational states come together in response to globalization and *thereby* develop their regional sovereignty and identity beyond the national level. They are thus cooperative and individual states – individual states *on the basis of cooperative states*. In other words, interstate unions open up new scope for action by postnational individual states.

For example, only Europe-wide initiatives make it possible to end fiscal dumping and to ask 'virtual taxpayers' to start paying up again. In this way, not only can the conditions be created for a social and ecological Europe, but individual states can also regain their capacity for action and their power to shape events. The question of why states should merge is thus answered by reference to state egoism: because only then can they renew their sovereignty within the framework of world society and the world market.

This argument makes sense only if the imaginative world of exclusive sovereignty is replaced with the imaginative world of *inclusive sovereignty*. A well-known case for the division of labour asserts that cooperation does not hinder but *develops* both the productivity and the sovereignty of the individual. Harking back to Durkheim's distinction, we might say that in interstate relations the *organic sovereignty of cooperation* replaces the mechanical anarchy of different natures. This means that national players *win* political room to shape events insofar as they increase economic and public wealth through transnational cooperation. Transnational states are therefore global *trading* states, which have bidden farewell to the priorities of geopolitical calculation along with the exclusive territorial principle.

The consequence is that war, so to speak, becomes a luxury that only national states isolated from one another can afford to wage – and even then, only if they do not fall within the sphere of influence of a military alliance and if they do not confront one another with the most modern instruments of force.[5]

The question of how to achieve a political architecture of transnational states may be answered by reference to two goals or pillars: the principle of a *pacifism enshrined in international law,*[6] and the *federalist* principle of interstate controls.[7]

The first principle states that, without the creation and expansion of international law and law courts, transnational conflicts cannot be settled by peaceful means.[8] This legal pacifism should be distinguished from what we might call *social pacifism* (which places the social causes of transnational conflicts at the centre of attention), as well as from *religious* pacifism (which aims at dialogue and equality between religions). Nor should legal pacifism be confused with freedom from violence: what it crucially implies is legally binding decisions with regard to the use of military force.

Now, the pillar of legal pacifism within a transnational order can only ever be a necessary but not sufficient condition for the peaceful resolution of conflicts. This is true of the resolution of conflicts both within and between national states. The history of the present century teaches us that the political fate of international courts is marked by a *paradox of success and failure*. For they have been successful when they have not actually been used; and they have always been unsuccessful when they have actually been used. The logical argument that a system of international law is indispensable conflicts with the sobering experience that states will fight over every inch of their remaining sovereignty, and will do so all the more doggedly the less there is to defend and the more there is to gain through joining together.

Today work is being done everywhere on the foundations of international law, and no one seriously doubts that this is necessary. But the results are very limited. It is true that the courts of justice in The Hague and Arusha have helped the prosecution of war criminals in the civil wars of the Balkans and Rwanda. But even in the case of Bosnia-Herzegovina, the Dayton Agreement has not made it possible to bring suspected war criminals such as Mladic, Karadzic or Kordic to trial and thereby to assist reconciliation and a new political beginning.

These failures, however, do not justify the conclusion that international law has no point. On the contrary, there are powerful reasons why transnational legal jurisdictions and institutions have long been a necessity for all states, and no longer just an optional luxury. For as more and more fields of action become global, national states may perhaps not surrender their legal power of decision, but they do lose control over enforcement of the law. Since individual states find themselves clutching at thin air (the thin air of the Internet, for example) in the collection of taxes, the fight against unemployment, or the war on economic crime, they are forced into transnational cooperation simply in order to enforce national law.

Here again we see the paradoxical principle of self-empowerment through self-deprivation of power. In order to increase their chances of asserting control, national states are forced to delegate their instruments of power to cooperative transnational authorities. Only in this way, as post-national states cooperating with others, can they renew and expand their capacity to influence events. As argued before, it is the state's own interests which compel it to give up its independent interests as a national state.

In fact, there is even a danger that the contradiction between national framework for action and transnational problems will lead to the hyperactive adoption of ever more national controls – controls which completely fail to address the problem they are supposed to solve but which also restrict and undermine the legal space for action.

Finally, national norms afford less and less security from all kinds of crime organized according to an international division of labour and with the help of global technology. Calls for national legislation that will give the state equal weapons to combat crime inevitably come faster and faster to nothing. Infringements of basic rights, such as the plans for optical and acoustic surveillance of the private domain which represent a grave risk to the rule of law and civic freedom, merely create the illusion that effective action will be possible; they do not permit any real fight against the kinds of crime in question, nor therefore do they actually make citizens any safer. It is only a matter of time before this shattering of the illusion of security further undermines confidence in the democratically legitimized order.[9]

Federalism, as applied to the relationship between states, has the decisive advantage that power is controlled, or at least held in check, neither from above nor from below but horizontally. A major problem is that the body which supervises individual states is not supposed to be a supra-state authority, since this would either be ineffective or be monopolized by the strongest and therefore ultimately lead to a world state. That would certainly be the most tyrannical of structures, from which no one would be able to escape in the end. It would also be extremely fragile, because it would replace diversity with uniformity and leave no room for conflict-resolving institutions.

Transnational federalism means a policy of active *self-integration* of individual states within international action contexts, so that they gain a new life as individual glocal states and limit the power of transnational centres. It is assumed that 'a democratic state is an imperfect political entity as long as there exist no institutions able democratically to link its citizens to the citizens of other states.'[10]

Let us sum up. *Inclusive sovereignty* means that the surrender of sovereignty rights is accompanied by a gain in the political power to mould events, on the basis of transnational cooperation. This will work out, of course, only if globalization is successfully conceived and shaped as a political project. Only then will it be possible for consent, employment, taxes and political freedoms all to grow both locally and transnationally. In this sense, Europe has become a laboratory experiment in inclusive sovereignty.[11]

Joint ownership of capital

If it is true that labour is being replaced by knowledge and capital, a new social policy *can set itself the goal of giving labour a share in capital*. The principle of joint ownership would then appear as a complement (or competitor?) to the principle of workforce participation in management. The models currently under discussion

range from the replacement of wage-interests by ownership interests (in enterprise capital, with its profits *and* losses) through to the
idea that Mercedes or Hoechst, for example, could produce wherever it was cheapest, while the Germans, as a 'nation of share-
holders', would live happily ever after from global dividends and
the proceeds of stock-exchange speculation.

'Parties and trade unions which still wish to pursue the goal of
fairer distribution,' writes Fritz W. Scharpf, 'must reorient their
efforts from tax and wages policy to the distribution of capital
assets.' But he immediately adds the restriction: 'In times of sharply rising real wages, such a goal would obviously be easier to
achieve than it is today. Besides it is now necessary to pay for the
fact that plans of this kind, when mooted by the Social Democrat–
Liberal coalition in the early seventies, withered under the polemic
of the trade unions against "people's capitalism".'[12]

The limits of such a policy are plain to see. To shift one's sights
from wages to income from capital offers support or security only
to those who are integrated into the labour process, not to the
unemployed who stand at the closed gates of the labour market.

Reorientation of educational policy

If labour is being replaced by knowledge and capital, the second
political conclusion is that labour must be revalued or reshaped by
knowledge. But this means *investing in education and research* – which
is not at all what is happening today in Germany.[13]

'Policy makers,' writes Robert B. Reich, 'have failed to understand that a nation's real technological assets are the capacities of
its citizens to solve complex problems of the future.' It is their
knowledge, their contribution to the world economy – and not, as
hitherto, technology and capital – which determine a country's
prosperity. 'Money, plants, information, and equipment are footloose. Brains, however, are far less mobile internationally.'[14]

Instead of subsidizing 'German' firms, politicians ought to invest
money in knowledge and training, so that citizens have the right
abilities and approaches to prosper in the transnational landscapes
and contradictions of world society.

One of the main political responses to globalization is therefore
to build and develop the education and knowledge society; to make
training longer rather than shorter; to loosen or do away with its
link to a particular job or occupation, gearing it instead to key

qualifications that can be widely used in practice. This should not
only be understood in terms of 'flexibility' or 'lifelong learning',
but should also cover such things as social competence, the ability
to work in a team, conflict resolution, understanding of other
cultures, integrated thinking, and a capacity to handle uncertain-
ties and paradoxes of the second modernity.[15]

'Learning should be associated with activities through which
people take their own lives in their hands,' writes Reinhard Kahl.
'Learning is being at once extended and freed from its ghetto.
Naturally this is easier said than done.'[16] However, the meaning
of learning changes within the transcultural nexus. It is part of the
exciting dialectic of globalization that it replaces traditional 'lectur-
ing societies' (Wolf Lepenies) with dialogic attentiveness and the
courage to disagree. Here and there people are beginning to sit up
and realize that something like a transnationalization of university
education and curricula will also be necessary ('global studies').
This should make it easier for students to understand and deal
with the difficulties of transnational communication and conflict.
And it should provide them with a cognitive map of the many
dimensions and traps of 'glocal' living and action.

In this age of individualization, it is no longer enough to support
young people in a 'flexible internalization of given norms' (Kohl-
berg). Something much deeper is required – what Michael Brater
calls 'the training of one's own self as a centre of action and
organization'. 'Today,' he continues, 'all young people have to
learn by themselves, through their own resources, to live their
own life – to learn and experiment, to shape an open process.'[17]

Are transnational corporations undemocratic or anti-democratic?

A transnational capitalism that pays no taxes and does away with
paid employment loses its legitimacy; it becomes, as Schumpeter
predicted, functionlessly parasitic. We must therefore now ask the
central question of the second modernity. Are the executives of
transnational corporations hostile to democracy? What value does
a refounding of democracy have for them?

How do 'virtual taxpayers' imagine the future of democracy?
What is their contribution to a cosmopolitan expansion of democracy?

What is the possible shape of a social contract that refounds and facilitates a democracy of the second modernity, looked at not (or not only) from the point of view of national politics but also from that of transnational corporations?

Maybe I am an incorrigible optimist; maybe this too is a strategic optimism. But it would be a straightforward, though momentous and perhaps suicidal, mistake to divorce the market economy from its originating context and, as it were, to pursue it in a bare and unvarnished state. The project of a market economy has always also been a political project, closely bound up with democracy. But democrÃcy is an expensive business. And there is no escaping the fact that the winners from globalization must be reminded of their responsibility for democratic institutions: that is, *the virtual tax-payers have to be asked to pay up.*[18]

This is not a German or European problem; it is a problem facing world society. It can be solved only through international regulation. Of course, transnational economic players are also dependent on the market and on their public image: they have an Achilles heel that makes them vulnerable. The limitless self-realization of capital must therefore be tied down, first to *places*, and second to *products*. Footloose capital must itself become 'sedentary' and adapt itself to local cultures and legal-political frameworks – which also means that it must justify itself within them;[19] produce goods and services that people will choose to buy, and are thus able to turn down.

What would a consumers' movement resembling Amnesty International or Greenpeace actually look like, one which not only used a *politicization of consumption* to encourage world corporations to maintain democratic standards, but which used the threat of boycotts to force them into it? To what extent can the politically alert, organized consumer – who has mastered the symbolic-political tools of the media – complement or replace the organized worker as a corrective to the limitless 'self-realization of capital'?

It has been said many times that, in comparison with attempts to pin down those responsible within the jungle of the world market, the fabled search for a needle in a haystack would be ridiculously easy. But this is not a correct way of arguing. The allocation of responsibility is never a matter of course; it always has to be *established*.

There is one very simple way of giving considerable political leverage to consumer movements that have only tiny levers at their disposal. Three things are required:

1   A duty to provide *legible markings that make a product easy to identify.*
2   *Social, democratic and environmental labels* indicating the conditions under which a product has been manufactured, and (voluntary) democratic commitment on the part of the producing firm.
3   *Product liability*, so that financial penalties are incurred if the information given is demonstrably incorrect.

This truly simple policy of product 'transparency' and liability, which involves no bureaucratic costs and is wonderfully compatible with corporate self-obligation and self-regulation, has been repeatedly attacked by representatives of business. How, they ask, are we to know the conditions of production of everything we sell? But this is precisely the point. Product liability makes it *compulsory* to be clear about such things, to respect the *minima moralia* of socially and environmentally aware production in dealings with one's business partners, in order to avoid one's own economic failure. Anyone who engages in world trade must be prepared to share world responsibility for the social and political conditions of such trade. This political response to globalization reconciles what appears irreconcilable: *local* regulation and corporate *self*-regulation.[20]

It is true that even social and environmental clauses are no panacea for the taming of the world economy. Their limitations are indeed self-evident. For they work mainly in relation to export-oriented branches and countries, and can – at best! – only indirectly contribute to a general orientation of societies towards greater social justice. Consideration would also have to be given to paradoxical side-effects.

An alliance for civil labour

To what extent can an alliance be forged between transnational capital and transnational politics to create and develop tendencies towards a civil society that is at once decentralized and transnational?

A new social contract would have to start from the fact that our labour has become so productive that we need less and less of it to produce more and more goods and services. The material-social integration of people through gainful employment is, to be sure, as important as it always has been, but no longer in just a single form. It should be considered whether the generally observable involvement of civil society Õn sociotopes and biotopes – its capacity for self-organization, but also its interest in political projects inadequately perceived by institutions – can be revalued so as to form a second centre of activity and integration alongside that of gainful employment: a centre of *public* or *civil* labour. What does this mean?[21]

Work that has so far been performed voluntarily for the elderly, disabled or homeless, for people with AIDS or the illiterate and excluded, as well as ecological commitments and much else besides, ought to be made economically visible and paid accordingly (for example, in the form of *civil money* at the same level as welfare payments). Civil labour could make the cities fit to live in: it could make energy expenditure more efficient and democracy more lively. Perhaps, instead of an 'alliance for labour', one could even speak of an alliance between citizens and the state for civil society, and try to attract capital behind it. Civil labour would have to appeal to everyone, and not just be a collecting tank for the unemployed. It would have to become a second centre of activity that made the democratic substance of society more secure. The point of it would be not to replace but to complement regular employment. In the end perhaps civil labour would become one of three foundations, together with paid employment (the main source of economic security) and work on one's own behalf (for the purposes of child-rearing or self-fulfilment). Instead of remaining within the national framework, civil labour might come to support and enrich transnational civil society and its various networks and social movements. As we can see from Greenpeace or Amnesty International, it is this kind of activity which most appeals to young people.

There are two principles, then – *voluntariness* or *self-organization*, and *public funding* – which could make civil labour an attractive proposition.[22]

All this immediately raises the question of where the money would come from. Here we will simply offer a few notes and ideas.

Income support and unemployment benefit According to the above model, the unemployed would in future have a choice between remaining unemployed and dependent upon welfare, and becoming active in the voluntary public sector. The various forms of transfer income could then be spent accordingly – quite independently of the fact that the unemployed people who took the second option would no longer be unemployed (and not simply be massaged out of the statistics).

Tax relief Just like the various registered associations which benefit from special dispensations, civil labour would also have to be exempted from income tax.

Charitable organizations Who distributes what to whom in this instance? And how could the resources in question become more transparent and be opened up for the funding of voluntary civil labour?

Non-monetary sources Exchange networks and coupon systems.

Social sponsoring Previously, transnational companies have found it good for their image to engage in the promotion of culture, and they have also taken up environmental issues. By now, there exists a veritable sponsorship movement within big corporations. A conscious public could thus hold them to their responsibilities, on the basis of the ground rules they have themselves laid down. Besides, I assume that managers consider the political freedom of this culture to be a valuable achievement, and that they would want to make their own contribution to it.

All this presupposes an understanding of politics that no longer accepts its monopolization by the political system. A new division of power and labour must be elaborated between, for instance, state-system politics and (trans)local civil society. To strengthen civil societies across frontiers does not mean to burden them, in the spirit of communitarian smooth talk, with every unresolved problem arising from bureaucratic lassitude. What it does mean is that a greater sense of responsibility for one's own affairs has developed together with the shift in power from the centre to the regions and municipalities. At the same time, civil money allows citizens' initiatives to stand on their own feet and to become capable of action.

No one should be blind to the fact that new problems are also incurred along the way. For example, there is constant rivalry among political parties and in town halls, and centres of self-organization within civil society often compete (much more expensively) with professional experts and employees. This gives rise to permanent conflict of various kinds over demarcation issues and other sources of friction.

What comes after the Volkswagen export nation? New cultural, political and economic goals

The overcoming of the division of Germany involves much more than incorporation of the GDR into the Federal Republic. As it is accompanied by the overcoming of the division of Europe, it spells the end of an epoch and the beginning of a new phase of European history.

What this entails, and what it presupposes, may be explained by reference to the understanding that postwar West Germany had of itself and of contemporary trends. At the time there were a number of optics that meshed together: reconstruction, internal democratization, suppression of any debate about the Nazi terror, struggle for reunification. These historical goals were far from constituting an obvious unity. Indeed, they tended to conflict with one another, permitting or even compelling different emphases and priorities. Nevertheless, they were all bound together by the project of making Germany an *export nation*.

The goal of mass-producing certain goods (Volkswagen, Mercedes, Siemens, etc.) and conquering world markets with 'German workmanship' concentrated cultural energies and cranked up the engine of wealth. It was this 'economic miracle' which laid the basis for internal democratization, for a reckoning with the organized mass murder of the Nazi period, and above all, of course, for reconstruction in both an inward and outward sense.

The Bonn Republic pursued this association of the goals of production and market conquest with a cultural-political drive to link up with Western modernity. Thus, the decisive source of legitimacy and consent was a *seemingly eternal more-of-everything*: affluent society, mass consumption, social security. Political freedom was subordinate to these.

More and more people, however, are now profoundly disturbed by the fact that the sources of affluence have begun to dry up or are bubbling forth in an extremely unequal pattern. Other goals – reconstruction, union with the GDR – have been achieved and exhausted or else become superfluous, facing us everywhere with the unexpected consequences of success. Still other goals have to be spelt out afresh for the new world situation.

Germany's conception of itself as an export nation – the reverse side of deutschmark nationalism – no longer carries much weight. One of the key challenges is the fact that the countries of South-

East Asia, and soon also China, can now produce just as well and more cheaply the goods that previously gave German brands their lead: cars, machinery, refrigerators. Furthermore, the markets for mass-produced goods have shifted to other parts of the world (South America, Eastern Europe, China, etc.), where they can now be serviced more cheaply on the spot. The result is again that the 'export nation' model of success is running out of steam. Or else the onward march of mass-produced goods – with the motor-car as the best example – has been called into question by an awareness of their ecological consequences.

In the manner of a prayer-wheel, 'innovations' and 'courage to take risks' are invoked by politicians and businessmen as the way to survive on the world market. But it suggests a thoroughly antiquated understanding of 'innovation' to continue betting on mass-produced goods and the export-nation model, so as to wad- dle along, with all the zest of a lame duck, behind what others can already do better and cheaper. The race to catch up on the so-called 'markets of the future' (information technology, genetic engineer- ing, human genetics), which is being so loudly trumpeted on all sides, is itself an expression of the prevailing blockages (including in thought) and the lack of fantasy. 'Innovation' in world society is a relational concept. It means being forced to invent and do what others are *not* (or not yet) able to do. One cannot keep ahead simply by longing to match others. The whole debate over 'loca- tional factors', much of it borrowed from military strategy, is blind or even *hostile* to innovation.

The real question, then, is what combination of culture, politics and economics could appear in place of the Volkswagen-exporting nation. Which innovations in marketing and culture can carry us forward into the second modernity? The world market rewards *difference*. So the point is to discover and develop, as a potential source of strength, things which have been condemned as, for example, regional peculiarities.

First, *ecological products*. One should not underestimate or dis- miss the popularity on the world market of the ecological con- science of the Germans. The orthodoxy of industrial society still prevailing in big corporations, but also among civil servants and in the major political parties, condemns the new ecological sensitivity of the Germans as a 'hindrance to innovation', instead of turning it into a world-market trump card for the second modernity. Some years ago, the president of the Federal Patents Office already pointed out that over 85 per cent of all inventions were not followed through in practice – not because they were uneconomic, but because their economic viability had been underestimated or never even tested. Company directors and politicians only think in the categories of high technology, genetic engineering and information technology, and focus on rolling back the competition in these sectors. In other words, they strive to establish innovation monopolies which others have been holding for a long time. Few today consider taking some of the risks for new products in order to open up new markets – a course still quite normal only twenty or thirty years back. Thus, in the coalition agreements for the twelfth legislative period of the German Bundestag (which began on 16 January 1991), the section on 'Environment and Transport' proclaimed the wonderful goals of 'replacing car taxes with a widely applied tax on harmful substances and CO_2 components', and of developing 'environmentally friendly fuels through the admixture of ethanol or biological lubricants'. But they have remained no more than good intentions.[23]

Second, *individualization*. Although attitudes to it are often negative, there is an opportunity to transform the local individualism of Western Europe into a competitive advantage on the world market, by developing highly individualized products and services, as well as related types of work and production that would probably also be labour-intensive, or anyway more labour-intensive. For the individualization of products and production is (within certain limits) the opposite principle to the automation of production. It also involves testing and inventing new combinations of services and products, such as organizational leasing and software capable of solving problems for firms and consumers.[24]

Third, *risk markets*. It has repeatedly been said that talk of a 'risk society' has rather German overtones of security and prosperity. At least since 'mad cow disease', however (which triggered a most infectious outbreak of institutional and political madness), it has become clearer that ignorance of risks takes not only a political but also an economic toll, *at the latest* by the selling stage. *Precarious* markets emerge in which consumers take flight at the first (always possible) reports of risk. Public risk-discourse, which is as dependable as the amen in church, *devalues* capital and forces companies throughout the world to take serious account, in their production of goods and services, of what consumers might think in the watchful countries of the West. This cannot be countered by any exporting of jobs and research departments to seemingly risk-blind parts of world society. For the situation can change with the speed of lightning: a single accident, or report of an accident, is enough. And besides, the products or services have to be sold to sup- posedly 'risk-hysterical' consumers in Western Europe.

One of the crucial questions of the second modernity is therefore how to win consumers' consent for risk-filled products and ser- vices (for example, genetically modified foodstuffs). Here social scientists have a contribution to make. A new German 'product image' might involve the testing and exporting of 'sets of products capable of gaining acceptance', so that, through new forms of participation and a transparent product policy, new products could be designed (and not just packaged) which would have an *acceptance-value* in addition to their use-value. Were this to happen, such 'acceptance-capable' products and forms of production would have a long-term superiority over others on the world market.[25]

Fourth, *re-regionalization of markets*.[26] Globalization presupposes lower transport and energy costs. Globalization is therefore obstructed – as a result of the boosting of regional markets for goods, services and labour – if the subsidies underpinning lower transport costs are withdrawn. If real energy and transport costs then increase (for example, through higher taxes or infrastructural charges), this will favour *a policy of short-distance regional markets*, and hence also more eco-friendly ways of working and living.

This political strategy may be combined with a policy in which the *biographies* of products become an integral part of them, so that each product has three components: use-value, price and a history of its origin and production. This would contain information on easy-to-read labels about the various conditions under which it was produced: ecological (for example, in areas free of chemicals), social (regulated work conditions, no child labour) and political (basic rights, trade unions). Then the much-vaunted responsible citizen would be able to decide how much he or she valued making the everyday act of purchase a political ballot over global forms of work and life. Since product biographies assume labour-intensive production, they should here too (for example, in the food industry and agriculture) have considerable effects on the labour market and employment. One response to globalization might thus be a twofold strategy of increasing real transport costs and introducing social-ecological product biographies, which together would help to strengthen regional markets or to place them on a new and more solid foundation.

Fifth, *an end to the blockages involved in the image of cultural homo- geneity*. It is these blockages, in fact, which make the 'export nation' ridiculously ill-adapted for the diversity of world society in the second modernity. Just to take a banal example from the small Lower Bavarian town of Straubing, children from twenty-four different countries of origin can now be found in the main school – yet in the minds of people, parties and government departments at national level, the fiction still prevails that Germany can avoid becoming a multicultural society and thus maintain the *ius sanguinis* with a good conscience.

> Citizenship is not a sweet that one slips to a child who has been good. Citizenship is not a sugary reward but the staple democratic fare. One should not be surprised, then, if deficiency symptoms appear when Germany's native foreigners are denied the bread of democracy. It cannot depend on race, religion, origin or belief who has civil rights in German society. Anyone who lives, works and pays taxes over a period of time belongs to it, because otherwise democracy cannot function. And if families belong to it, then children born and bred here belong to it all the more. [...] True, there is a trend among young people (fairly independent of nationality) which ought to make one think about how they can be better integrated. This problem has been described only under the very academic heading 'social exclusion of adolescent marginal groups'. The reality consists of indifference and aggression at school, slashed car tyres, a climate of general insecurity and overstretched municipal authorities. The demand that foreigners' children born in Germany should not be allowed to become German, so that they can later be deported more easily, is a sad example of such overstretching.
>
> How many generations of so-called foreigners will have to be born here before they are finally recognized as citizens and treated as Germans? It is a question not of favours but of something that should be taken for granted in a democracy.[27]

Experimental cultures, niche markets and the self-renewal of society

Individualization means many things, but not the often-predicted doom of all values. Rather, it means that values become more differentiated, and personal autonomy self-evident and inescapable.[28] Last but not least, it means that *cultural sources have emerged for the joyful and creative taking of risks*.[29] These are able and determined to prove themselves on the market, in a new sense free of misguided bureaucratic mollycoddling. We can study examples of this today in a milieu of the future: *the only seemingly egoistic 'life-aesthetes'*.

'L'état, c'est moi. Every life-aesthete is an aristocrat', write Johannes Goebel and Christoph Clermont in their unpublished book 'Die Tugend der Orientierungslosigkeit' [The Virtue of Dis-orientation], which describes the outlook of the '89 generation.

> He rules his self-created princedom as an absolute sovereign. His life is not mainly concerned with worldly goals and the active morality of the bourgeoisie, but with the shaping of his own domain. His actions spring not from the pleasure principle but from a sense of duty to his own code of honour. His aim is to perfect existence, providing it with a more appropriate contemporary decor and a glorious stage-produced history.
>
> For the life-aesthete, then, work is not an end in itself, nor leisure time an oasis of self-fulfilment. Rather, he has an all-encompassing sense of responsibility to the tokens of his worth that he has himself chosen. The knights of neomodernity hold sway over a realm that contains no more than one person, yet the means of shaping this dominion are potentially limitless. Their round table is globally networked, their palaces can take in whole continents.
>
> In Germany, assets to the value of 2.6 billion marks will be inherited between now and the year 2006. This really does open the possibility for sizeable layers to renounce an economically active life and to devote their (in most cases, admittedly rather modest) existence to the realization of aesthetic lifestyle imperatives, instead of having to hail the exigencies of wage labour as the meaning of life. Moreover, the increasing support that parents give to their offspring's activity for an unprecedented number of years, and even the insecure 'Macjob' that requires no identification beyond the earning of some money, also tend to make the life-aesthete independent of the economy.
>
> Aristocratic existence is pre-economic. So long as a living is in some way or other assured, economic considerations are irrelevant. This does not mean, of course, that economic mechanisms are completely alien to the thinking of the life-aesthete, but only that he has left behind the sphere of lifelong employment. For him, economics no longer has anything to do with the earning of money; he sees it as a much more inclusive model of processes of calculation and negotiation, which is always necessary when he comes into contact with other aristocrats. Economics is the foreign trade of a principality that is otherwise governed according to the irrational principles of the divine right of lifestyle aesthetics.

However great is his sovereignty in internal affairs, the life-aesthete cannot and does not wish to gain control over the constructed world of his fellow humans. And so, the world of the life-aesthete completely lacks that indispensable pendant of lordship which is the servant. The only relevant model of human coexistence is the one of diplomacy between sovereign rulers.

So long as the norms of chivalry were maintained, the aristocrat's morality was utilitarian. The romantic bourgeois longing for wholeness was completely alien to him. And just as the decadent noble was a figure of loathing for the moralistic bourgeoisie of the eighteenth century, so all too often is the new morality of the life-aesthete uncomprehendingly confused with a collapse of values and egoistic opportunism.

Life-aesthetes are thus petty despots who have established a nation that grounds their own identity. This nation takes good care of their history (childhood, personal biography) and proudly presents its distinctive symbols, flags, coats of arms and uniforms (housing, style, etc.). So long as the borders are left untouched, the life-aesthete lives in peaceful coexistence with his neighbours, without being all that drawn to friendship with them. Ad hoc alliances to achieve some clear-cut goal are obviously not excluded. Only if there is a threat of foreign rule or conquest (imposition of someone else's will, institutional coercion) do peaceful communities become solemn defensive leagues. Daily border checks warn the rulers of situations that might endanger the smooth functioning of their rule. Burnt homes of asylum-seekers, environmental disasters, wars and crises all around the world are examined for their potential to damage the life-aesthete's project. If it comes to it, the little cabinets opt for a general mobilization, reach for the candle to keep intruders away, and organize boycotts or demonstrations. These blue-helmet missions of the sovereign life-aesthetes are, of course, short-lived operations. Once the threat recedes, the commitment does not take long to wane. But the mechanism can always be relied upon![30]

The social milieu of life-aesthetes – which is not so small and will perhaps set styles in general for the next generation – has become the everyday laboratory of civilization. Artists whose great work is their own life are not only inventive in protecting their distinctive traits. They also constantly practise the coordination of conflicting yet autonomous lifestyles, and they mould and stage both themselves and their own lives as an aesthetic product. Since living, thinking and producing are here in a direct association between work for oneself and work for others, the resulting markets do not have a mass character but are niches or mini-markets. It is a prejudice, however, that these special markets must always remain minimal in size. The opposite is the case. In the age of global localities, these special market-niche cultures are inventive bio-topes from which the chief designers of world-market products steal – or, to put it more nicely, 'create' – their ideas (for example, in the rai music scene).

At the same time, the *generalization of niche markets* with regional roots (markets which therefore have to be freed from the jungle of regulations and consciously promoted by political means!) is one of the central responses to the ending of the two great features of the first modernity: mass production and full employment.

Furthermore, to put it in a nutshell, the self-development motif operates as a *self-exploitation* motif. People are prepared to do a great deal for very little money, precisely because economic advantage is individualistically refracted and even assigned an opposite value. If an activity has greater value in terms of identity and self-fulfilment, this makes up for and even exalts a lower level of income.

Niche culture and niche production may present a countermodel to the rationalization mania prevalent in big capital. For they involve labour-intensive activities (products, services) with a limited but still high value in terms of meaningfulness and the future – and with low productivity and low earnings compensated by a multiplicity of further activities.

Niche production (a) makes possible a cultural laboratory of the future and an inventive mode of production, (b) does this with low production costs, and by relying upon independent initiatives (without grand bureaucratic schemes to shape the future) which (c) presuppose and strengthen regional specificities and the trans-national self-organization of civil society.

This runs completely counter to the know-all approach of adults defending the old values and world order, who seek to clip the wings of a generation of artists (grandchildren of the postwar economic miracle!) pursuing ironical self-discovery, and to bind them to a functionalist cog-wheel existence within the hierarchical and bureaucratic machinery. Their aim in this is to burn up the cultural riches of lifeworld creativity which the 'gentle young' represent and produce, and no doubt it would indeed exhaust and exclude the key milieu for the self-renewal of contemporary society.

Social entrepreneurs, people working for themselves

In place of the social figure of the wage-earning employee facing the capitalist employer, the picture now emerging is one in which there are *people working for themselves* on one side, and *social entrepreneurs* on the other. The person working for himself knows that he must no longer, and can no longer, simply carry out work given him by others in fulfilment of their bounden duty (any failure to do so being an error on their part, not his). He acts in the knowledge that 'his' work always has to be found and justified, in the sense of a socially enlarged use-value where all three components – social, use and value – are conceptualized together. This assumes a strong identification both with the needs of others and with the work. In this sense, work for oneself always implies both work in itself and work for others.

There is also a capitalist side, of course, the *entrepreneur* who 'manages' himself and his capacity for work. Andreas Zielcke writes as follows:

> The mass metamorphosis of employees into entrepreneurs is already in full swing. And it shows that, however coarse the consequences may be, the new powers of the market do not involve a return to the Wild West of early capitalism. Contemporary capitalism employs a method of valorization far more astute, complex and cynical than anything its comparatively crude forefathers could imagine.
>
> Early capitalism was based upon the exploitation of labour, while today's capitalism is based upon the exploitation of responsibility. Formerly workers had to help shape the object of their labour; now they have to help shape the company's results. Formerly they had only to work together with others; now they have to think and worry as well. Formerly they were like another cog in the production process; now the production process depends upon their involvement. The exploitation of others, which was always precarious and productive of resistance, is being replaced by a system of skimming the cream from theoretically limitless self-exploitation. Big companies are thus widely engaged in breaking up their prescribed internal channels, in order to spread the powers of decision-making among the available brains. Not only are decentralized units of profit being created; even individual work-teams have to justify their economic performance rather than a working plan.

Whether parts of jobs are 'outsourced' to contractors or subcon-
tractors, or whether, on the contrary, outside suppliers are linked
into the company's conveyor belt, the same primacy attaches to the
levelling of responsibility. This is also true of 'franchising'. A world
corporation such as McDonald's does not consist only of a small
hard core. The retail outlets of its planetary network are entrusted to
the ownership of countless individual operators, and headquarters
merely hands out its named licences, its know-how and its appropriate foodstuffs in return for a share in the proceeds. Employer
becomes licence-holder, employee turns into licensee. The company
philosophy holds that both sides – the big and the little entrepreneur
– gain higher profits from this combination of unity and atomiza-
tion.

All these synchronous processes of internal splitting and privati-
zation already make it possible to group together radical experiences of profit-related individual responsibility in a grey area
between dependence and independence. To an increasing extent,
big companies produce not only masses of commodities but also
masses of virtual entrepreneurs.[31]

A social contract against exclusion?

But are these not all fine-weather pictures of a society in the niche
of prosperity, which seem curiously old-fashioned in the present
stormy weather (nearly 5 million *registered* unemployed in Germany in the summer of 1997)? When today's reality is one of
growing poverty and urban decay, is not talk of creative 'niche
culture' and transnational 'civil society' perhaps a thing of the
past? Do they not assume an elementary security that we will not
be mugged or have our throat cut round the next street-corner? Is
this not the reason for the scarcely concealed irrationalism, the
propensity to violence, which exist not only on the margins of
society but at its very centre?

First, the income scissors have been opening wider. Over the last
fifteen years, real income from work has risen by 2 per cent
(practically not at all), while income from capital has soared by
59 per cent.[32] This marks only the beginning of a phase in which
the productivity of capital is growing without labour. In the global
age, labour kept becoming cheaper and more plentiful, capital
scarcer and more expensive. The declining return on labour and
the increasing return on capital thus led to an ever sharper division
between a world of the poor and a world of the rich.

Second, more and more groups are (at least temporarily) affected by unemployment and poverty. In the industrial heartlands of the West, a new 'lumpenproletariat' has emerged, an ever larger group of people *excluded from society*. This sociological concept of exclusion indicates the poverty trap at the heart of modern society: *no job without a fixed residence, no fixed residence without a job, no democracy without a job and somewhere to live.*

In the last two decades, world output has risen by 4,000 billion dollars to reach a total of 23,000 billion dollars – yet over the same period the numbers of the poor have risen by more than 20 per cent. The share of the poorest fifth of humanity in world income fell from 4 to 1 per cent between 1960 and 1990. By contrast, 358 dollar billionaires possess more than what a half of humanity put together currently earns.[33] Even if this attracts little attention, more than 35,000 children die every day around the world – not from typhoons or floods or other natural disasters, but from diseases of civilization that are relatively easy to prevent or cure with suitable care and treatment (pneumonia, diarrhoea, chicken-pox, malaria, tetanus, whooping cough). In two days, then, more children die than Americans were killed throughout the Vietnam War (58,000).[34]

In Germany today, more than 7 million people live in the shadows of prosperity, and even the seemingly secure middle layers are threatened with a drop in income. In the United States as in other European countries, this opening of the scissors between rich and poor, both within and between countries, cannot be underestimated in the effect it has on social and political events. And at the top levels of the economy and politics, the guessing-game is about *how much poverty a democracy can tolerate.*

Third, poverty and unemployment correspond less and less to class stereotypes: they are ever more difficult to identify and, therefore, to organize into a political force. Not only unemployment but also divorce, sudden illness, notice to quit a still reasonably priced flat, or the termination of a loan, are typical ways in which people fall into poverty and homelessness.

Fourth, in individualized types of existence, people have to accept individual responsibility (often including sole financial responsibility) for things that used to be treated by the community as a class destiny rather than a personal one. 'One is no longer a person. The loss of face is indescribable,' writes an East German unemployed man about the wretchedness of his existence. In the newly added regions of Federal Germany, this spectre of unemployment has by now directly or indirectly caught most people in its grip. That loss of a job means 'loss of face' is true there in a particularly profound sense. For the GDR was most emphatically a 'workers' society', where people were integrated into the community at their little place of work (often even after they had left to retire).

It is important to distinguish between situations of biographical insecurity which still appear to individuals as susceptible to calculation and control, and those which *no longer* appear so. The former belong to what I call risk biography, the latter to *danger* biography.

It is not easy to differentiate these gradations of socially produced existential insecurity. The grey areas are large and opaque, since the border is itself nothing other than its perception from the point of view of individuals. It is possible to list objective indicators, resources and yardsticks of normality, but none of them can hide the fact that the border between still-calculable risk biography and incalculable danger biography is an open gateway to subjective thinking, supposition, expectation, hope and prophecies of doom.

It has to be said, however, that if a growing number of people are for whatever reason prostrated by conditions they do not have the means to understand and to tame or ignore, this is a fact of great significance for the whole of society (and social analysis). The compulsion to self-activity and self-organization can suddenly turn into despair, perhaps also into dumb rage. The perception of danger biographies provides the fuel for violence and neo-nationalism and revolutions.

But what is to be done, if we are not to end our days (without suffering?) in a state of misery?

A number of different approaches and strategies have already been outlined in this book. The nature and genesis of the problem have also been repeatedly addressed. We might call it *the dilemma of social policy in the age of globality*: economic development *escapes the reach* of national politics, whereas the resulting social problems *cluster* in the safety-net of the national state. A prognosis of hard times ahead is obvious enough. For the number of conflicts over questions of allocation and income-distribution looks set to rise, *and* there is growing pressure for unpopular political decisions that will have to be tackled.

No one has come up with an answer to the key question of the second modernity: *How is social justice possible in the global age?* The next question – Can there be anything like a transnational system of social protection? – is also difficult to answer and will be the object of heated debate over the coming years.[35] There is no point in arguing against a world state and a world system of social security, because these are anyway not really impending. Pragmatically, the task is rather:

1   to establish and develop basic measures of social protection;
2   to strengthen social networks of self-provision and self-organization; and
3   to raise and keep alive world issues of social and economic justice in the centres of global civil society.

Aid in matters small and large, locally and in other continents, is often seen as part of a pluralist competition involving the miseries of homelessness, Alzheimer's disease, damage to the environment, and so on. Under the title 'Abschied vom Jammertal' [Farewell to the Vale of Tears], Veit Post, spokesman for German World Hunger Relief, objects to this way of looking at things.

> It is regrettable and unnecessary. For the work of most aid organizations is better than the reputation of development politics. Development aid, both public and private, has many successes to show for itself, some of which can be corroborated in figures. [...] It is much too defensive to argue that verifiable successes rest upon major assumptions: upon competence, professionalism and above-average motivation on the part of those working for aid organizations.
>
> Nine out of ten Germans think that development aid is necessary. Hundreds of thousands donate a total of some hundred million marks every year for this purpose, and schoolchildren display growing interest in the living conditions of people in the Third World. Are there better foundations on which to gain people's enthusiasm for development politics?
>
> If aid organizations want to lift the issue out of the vale of tears, they must learn to support rather than lecture; to offer better solutions rather than just name problems; to win people's hearts and not 'only' their understanding. They must show a capacity for action that goes beyond publishing more studies; they must be prepared for conflict, instead of eyeing up state donors; and they must think of themselves less as imparting a morality than as providing a service.
>
> The results of a private survey made among friends in Africa suggest that the concept of a 'vale of tears' cannot be adequately translated into their language.[36]

6

Europe and Globalization

Many are tortured by the remarkably essentialist question: What *is* Europe? Not uncommonly the answer states what Europe *was*. 'There can be no return to Europe, for the simple reason that Europe only exists in the museum of rhetoric.'[1]

Nevertheless, Europe is not a geographical but an *imagined* area. To the question of what constitutes Europe's identity, Milan Kundera, for example, replies: 'It pleases me to think that the art of the novel came into the world as the echo of God's laughter. [...] There is a fine Jewish proverb: Man thinks, God laughs. Inspired by that adage, I like to imagine that François Rabelais heard God's laughter one day, and thus was born the idea of the first great European novel.'[2]

Any number of other definitions are conceivable – for instance, the *European cosmopolitanism* that Montaigne, Goethe and Kant (to name but three) described and lived in their own lives, and which, after the catastrophe of Nazi Germany for European Jews and others, is today at home everywhere, including in Israel. All these definitions are existentially and politically indispensable for the future identity of Europe in the age of globalization.

But the question remains: Is political Europe not just an illusion? Anyone who takes the trouble to study the volumes of conference complaints that Europe does not exist, or that it is just coming into existence, will hardly be able to keep from yawning. There is no better bedtime reading – more effective than any sleeping pills and without their side-effects!

The confusing thing is that not only does a political Europe not exist; its very non-existence is not yet really experienced as a deficiency. Even committed intellectuals, who stand with quills at the ready to add their name as an embellishment to appeals for good and against evil, find themselves unable to intervene in 'European affairs' across the walls between individual states that still divide public opinion.

There is, for example, no real European newspaper. Nor is there a European television programme worthy of the name (that is, which grips its European audience to such an extent that national programmes slip down the table of viewing figures). Single-market Europe seems to have promoted the petty and provincial rather than the Europe-wide. And in these troubled times, people cling to snatches of the old and familiar, so as not to be swept away by the swirling rapids of 'everything is changing'.

But is it perhaps not the case that the moaning and groaning about Europe's political flop stems from falsely utopian ideas about what 'political Europe' should be?

Those who complain that a European political space has not yet arisen are really saying that there is no United States of Europe comparable to the United States of America, no European parliament, no European public sphere that deserves the name, no European political nation-state. Even visionary hopes can provide only scant cover for this bare nothing.

But is it feasible to make political Europe follow the conceptual schema of a national public sphere – at a historical moment when the national framework is breaking down and local-global identities are coming to the fore? Does 'being European' make it possible or impossible to identify with the excluded population of Brazil's *favelas*? As a European, can I feel associated with Greenpeace (including in its capacity as a deputy rubbish-sorter on a world scale)? Does 'Europe' repress my feminist self-awareness? Or does a European identity strengthen both feminist and ecological identity? What is one actually for or against when one is also, or mainly, for or against Europe?

All these questions make it clear that no one is waiting for Europe. It is only an add-on that has to struggle for attention. For the time being, Europe is no more than a label, a car sticker, or one more bureaucratic prescription.

Why Europe? Why not Helga or grandma or the homeless across the street or on the other side of the world? In future this question must be answered by *Europeans*. What is at issue when Europe is being talked about? Milk price subsidies? An *exclusive* 'fortress Europe'? Or an *inclusive* Europe that conceives of itself as the political tamer, the active political moulder, of economic globalization? The crucial first insight is that *without Europe there can be no response to globalization*. What Europe is or should be, then, cannot be conjured up from the past; it has to be developed as a political response to the questions of the future, in every field such as the labour market, ecology, the social state, international migration, political freedoms and basic rights. Only in the transnational space of Europe can the politics of individual countries change from a threatened object to a shape-giving subject of globalization.

But then it has to be asked what answers a political Europe – and *only* a political Europe – can give to the challenges of the global age.

'I share the reservation,' says Joschka Fischer, 'that Europe is being built around a bank. The only question is what consequences are drawn from this. I too wanted to see as the first step not Maastricht but a process of political integration. But should we therefore call off this first real transfer of sovereignty at a European level? I would consider that to be wrong.' For first, Fischer continues, the debate over introduction of the euro

> is being conducted in similar terms in every national society. There is an advantage in this. Perhaps, for the first time, a European debate will even emerge out of the internal politics of the respective national cultures. Second, the European labour market throws up more and more problems because of its lack of regulation. Portuguese construction workers are introduced here and African construction workers in Portugal, while German construction workers are unemployed. For the first time, this is leading to debate about whether one should turn back and tighten the borders again, or else take a step forward and contemplate regulation of the European labour market as such. Third, during the Mururoa confrontation in 1995, Chirac had to recognize that European integration has advanced quite a bit since 1965 and the times of de Gaulle. Atomic weapons testing could no longer be taken for granted. I hope these three points will make it clear that a European debate is beginning to take place around the construction of a euro-currency. It may prove useful, not in keeping the focus on a bank, but in achieving a European discussion of constitutional matters. We need a European definition of basic law.[3]

There is no national way out of the global trap. But there is a transnational one: a transnational structure as large as the European Union could restore the primacy of politics, could make it possible for participating states to engage in democratically accountable action on issues of social and economic policy. In reality, a strong and democratic European Union could use its weight as the world's largest trading power to achieve real reforms – both externally and internally. The World Trade Organization would have to be thoroughly reformed again, and minimum social and ecological standards would have to be urgently introduced. This would not be for protectionist reasons, but to go beyond Europeans' dual morality according to which the human values defined and protected by Europe do not apply to people in other countries. The policy of deregulating transnational organizations would thus be countered with a demand for *re*-regulation, for the reintroduction of social and ecological standards. We need a uniform tax system in the European Union, not another set of loopholes. The aim should be to achieve balanced world trade, so that it is no longer the case that ever fewer people make ever higher profits while everyone else foots the bill. Finally, we must open up debate on a Europe-wide ecological tax reform and counter the arguments of those opposed to it within various countries. We must help other countries to produce for their *own* market, so that their *own* population become more involved. Globalization, as we have said, means re-regionalization at both a sub-national and a supranational level.

A policy list of presents for Father Christmas to bring – that is one utopian way of describing what we have just outlined. M. Greffrath offers a list of his own:

A society where time is set free, a social system that cautiously reorients itself to independent citizens' activity, an active state that consciously uses demand to promote and guide industrial innovation (which technological system do we want in the future? which does the world want?), a Europe that does not seal itself off but organizes exchange with neighbouring regions and the world market, a worldwide taming of the multinationals – any more wishes? Yes, of course. A society of freed time, and a Europe that perceives its 'second chance' (Habermas) and sorts out some of the things with which it has enriched and overtaxed the world during the past four hundred years – this naturally assumes little short of a cultural revolution, events no less great than those of the Renaissance. It is

absurd to summon them up. But somehow it occurs to one that a
change of seasons may be playing its part, as if a few swallows are
already flying around up there. When the world's top speculator
says that liberal finance-capitalism is more dangerous than communism was in its time, or when the luxury goods producer Joop
says that he would not personally keep any of the trash he churns
out and that he thoroughly despises the people who adorn themselves with it, then a change of values is blowing in the wind – even
if these mild forms of dissidence are not yet of the Sakharov type.
And with this comes the possibility of a change of elites. Small
beginnings are in the air when the Volkswagen workers in Wolfs-
burg are content with less money and their wives are very content;
when the owner of a great machine-tool factory (like most of his
colleagues) dreams of a general reduction in working time – 'only
everyone has to do the same'; when Jürgen Schrempp loudly
denounces the lack of European planning to German bankers and
calls for the building of high-speed routes to Moscow in order to
create jobs, profits and European spirit; when Swabian businessmen
go into raptures over a major initiative to provide the great cities of
South-East Asia with ecologically sound transport solutions; and
when Paul Kennedy calmly expects that 'Europe' will clean up the
Mediterranean. At a time when the world is being reorganized,
when large-scale systems are dissolving or stagnating, people search
for new paths. At first these are individual, only half-legal fiddles.
And for a time, what the old administrators do is less important
than how many individuals strike out in new directions. Temporarily, there seem to be no real bridges between the demands
expressed in the big books of analysis, and the everyday lives of
trainees, casual workers or students. A different politics will come
only when a government risks admitting in public that the market
no longer sorts things out. Only then can there be a New Deal:
between the generations, between the jobless and the employed,
between the sexes, and between state and society.[4]

Conclusion

Decline à la Carte: The Brazilianization of Europe

If this New Deal does not happen, if the fatalistic attitudes of postmodernism and neoliberal globalism become a self-fulfilling prophecy, then doom really will be on the agenda. The nightmare scenarios that are already on nearly everyone's mind could then certainly become reality. Let us use the conventional shorthand for one of these and imagine what the *Brazilianization of Europe* would be like.

The neoliberals have won, even against themselves. The national state has been cleared away. The social state is in ruins. But it is not a non-order which prevails. In place of the legal and power structures of national players, there are many conflicting units of rule that set themselves up as separate and fight against one other. Between them are a number of legal and normative no-man's-lands.

In the dangerous inner cities, employees wearing ties live and work in video-monitored edifices that have been closely packed together according to the old fortress principle. These are veritable castles, equipped and ruled by transnational corporations.

Nearby there are parks and nature reserves occupied by militant Greens (so-called 'terrorist germs') and defended by force of arms.

In some areas, drugs are freely advertised and consumed. In others, cigarette-smoking already carries the death penalty. Armed pensioners regularly patrol the borders of their well-maintained settlements.

There are expressways for super-limousines, but in their eternal roundabout they have to satisfy each other's flashing-light requests to overtake – something that the sporty little numbers hardly notice.

Moreover, these roads border on cycling districts where *not* to travel by bike is severely punished – with all the conflicts that break out daily as a result. For all have to answer this conundrum in their own way: How can I get off my bicycle without, at least momentarily, breaking the law that forbids being a pedestrian? In these districts, the steps and staircases have been designed so that bicycles can negotiate them, and both marriage beds and writing desks have pinned beside them official advice on how to position vehicles and how to switch in a non-pedestrian manner to other of life's functions (such as sleeping and working). Not perfect, but then nor is life.

Public means of transport are under a cloud, because they recall the dinosaurs of the national state. Their insignia can in fact only be visited in well-guarded museums.

Those who enter the still-functioning underground lay themselves wide open to attack, so that to be mugged is tantamount to putting oneself in the dock. The rule is that people who are mugged are themselves guilty of being mugged.

Between these unclearly differentiated jurisdictions of companies, associations, drug cartels, salvation armies, militant naturalists and cycling societies, on the one hand, and opportunities to let oneself be voluntarily robbed, on the other (perhaps because one's therapist thinks it necessary for one's personal development), there is no more than a distant memory of that proud nation-state for which people riddled one another with bullets and blew one another up by the million. States represent particular interests among those who have particular interests.

If one takes any transnational corporation – the 'Deutsche Bank', for example, which is now called the 'World Bank' – it becomes clear that the power relationship has been reversed. One has to put a little statelet under a magnifying glass to recognize it; whereas corporations have to be looked at through the wrong end of a telescope if one is to see them at all.

Similarly, in place of the United Nations, an organization has appeared which calls itself United Coca-Cola – or something like that.

The remnants of the state also raise taxes, or should one say: they make demands for taxes. So it goes. But tax payments have, at least de facto, long been a matter of voluntary contributions, as it were. Besides, they have to be creamed off and allocated in competition with all the other protection money and tributes that the units of personal rule demand with the help of their gun-toting security services. For the state's monopoly of violence, like all other monopolies, has been abandoned. What remains is an essay at an external policy. But seldom has the honorary title 'Essay', which used to be commonly found only in bookshops, been as appropriate as it is here.

Further Reading

Albrow, M., *The Global Age*, Cambridge 1995.

Appadurai, A., 'Disjuncture and Difference in the Global Cultural Economy', in M. Featherstone, ed., *Global Culture: Nationalism, Globalization, and Modernity*, London 1990.

Archibugi, D., 'From the United Nations to Cosmopolitan Democracy', in D. Held, ed., *Cosmopolitan Democracy: An Agenda for a New World Order*, London 1995.

Archibugi, D., Held, D. and Köhler, M., eds, *Re-imagining Political Community: Studies in Cosmopolitan Democracy*, Cambridge 1999.

Bauman, Z., *Globalization*, Cambridge 1998.

Beck, U., *World Risk Society*, Cambridge 1999.

—— 'Democracy Beyond the Nation-State', *Dissent*, winter 1999.

—— *The Brave New World of Work*, Cambridge 2000.

—— 'The Cosmopolitan Perspective. On the Sociology of the Second Age of Modernity', *British Journal of Sociology*, 1, 2000.

Bretherton, C. and Ponton, G., eds, *Global Politics*, Oxford 1996.

Castells, M., *The Rise of the Network Society*, Oxford 1996.

Cerny, P. G., 'Globalization and the Changing Logic of Collective Action', *International Organization*, 49, 1995.

Eade, J., ed., *Living the Global City*, London, 1997.

Elkins, D. J., *Beyond Sovereignty: Territory and Political Economy in the Twenty-first Century*, Toronto 1995.

Giddens, A., *Beyond Left and Right*, Cambridge 1994.

—— *The Third Way: The Renewal of Social Democracy*, Cambridge 1998.

Gilpin, R., *The Political Economy of International Relations*, Princeton 1987.

Habermas, J., *Die postnationale Konstellation*, Frankfurt/Main 1998.

Held, D., *Democracy and the Global Order*, Cambridge 1995.

Held, D. et al., *Global Transformations*, Cambridge 1999.

Hirst, P. and Thompson, G., *Globalization in Question*, Cambridge 1996.

Kapstein, E. B., 'Workers and the World Economy', *Foreign Affairs*, May–June 1996.

Lash, S. and Urry, J., *The End of Organized Capitalism*, Cambridge 1987.

—— *Economies of Signs and Space*, London 1994.

McGrew, A., 'A Global Society?', in S. Hall et al., eds, *Modernity and its Futures*, Cambridge 1992.

—— ed., *The Transformation of Democracy*, Cambridge 1997.

Miller, D. (ed.), *Worlds Apart. Modernity Through the Prism of the Local*, London, New York 1995.

Pieterse, J. N., 'Globalization as Hybridization', in M. Featherstone, S. Lash and R. Robertson, eds, *Global Modernities*, London 1995.

Robertson, R., *Globalization: Social Theory and Global Culture*, London 1992.

—— 'Globalization', in M. Featherstone, S. Lash and R. Robertson, eds, *Global Modernities*, London 1995.

Rosenau, J., *Turbulence in World Politics*, Brighton 1990.

Shaw, M., *Civil Society and the Media in Global Crises*, London 1996.

Toulmin, S., *Cosmopolis: The Hidden Agenda of Modernity*, New York 1990.

Zolo, D., *Cosmopolis: Prospects for World Government*, Cambridge 1997.

Notes

Introduction

1 See A. Giddens, *Beyond Left and Right*, Cambridge 1994.
2 On the concept of 'subpolitics', see U. Beck, *The Reinvention of Politics*, Cambridge 1997, ch. 3.
3 *Le Monde diplomatique*, April 1997, quoting *Fortune*, 5 August 1996.
4 *Der Spiegel*, 12, 1997, pp. 92–105, which also contains figures on the sharp rise in profits accompanied by dramatic downsizing of the workforce.
5 An interview with André Gorz, *Frankfurter Allgemeine Zeitung*, 1 August 1997, p. 35.
6 See below, pp. 55ff.
7 U. Beck, 'Väter der Freiheit', in id., ed., *Kinder der Freiheit*, Frankfurt/Main 1997, pp. 377ff.
8 *Pater semper incertus*. An unforgiving dispute has broken out in the press over the paternity of the term 'second modernity'. Not to have read and not to be able to quote are not, however, sufficient grounds for originality – and suspicions. 'Zweite Moderne' [Second Modernity] is the title of a series edited by myself. And 'Auf dem Weg in eine andere Moderne' [Towards a New Modernity] was the subtitle of my book *Risk Society* (London 1992), which first appeared in German in 1986. Already a distinction is drawn there between 'simple' and 'reflexive' modernization, a 'first' and a 'second' modernity – as in each of my books that came after it. *The Reinvention of Politics* (Cambridge 1997), which first appeared in German in 1993, was originally intended to have the title *Jenseits von Links und Recht* [Beyond Left and Right], and then *Zweite Moderne* [Second Modernity]; both were subsequently rejected for various reasons. Now, it may be true that the meaning one gives to a concept plays only a marginal role, but even in terms of content there is a great similarity between *second modernity* and *new* or *different modernity*. The themes of the book series I have been editing – individualization, ecological crisis, society without work, even

globalization itself – were already central themes of *Risk Society*. (I know that the next complaint will be: 'Aha, so there's nothing new!') If there is a conceptual elective affinity, then it is with the expression coined by Jürgen Habermas, 'uncompleted modernity'. See also J. Habermas, 'Jenseits des Nationalstaats?', in U. Beck, ed., *Politik der Globalisierung*, Frankfurt/Main 1997.

 9 See below, pp. 38f., 47f., 68–70, 88–93. See also U. Beck, 'The Cosmopolitan Perspective. On the Sociology of the Second Age of Modernity', *British Journal of Sociology*, 1, 2000.
10 Wallerstein's 'world-system' analysis is discussed below, pp. 31–4.
11 This is stressed by the group around David Held. See D. Held, *Democracy and the Global Order*, Cambridge 1995, pp. 99–136.
12 See below, pp. 108–13 and 132–6.

Part I Dimensions, Controversies, Definitions

1 For details see Kommission für Zukunftsfragen, *Zweiter Bericht*, Bonn 1997.
2 On the multiple meanings of the 'globalization' concept, see Paul Hirst and Grahame Thompson, *Globalization in Question*, Cambridge 1996, pp. 1–18.
3 Friedhelm Hengsbach, 'Wettlauf der Besessenen', interview in *Der Spiegel*, 10, 1997, p. 40.
4 See below, pp. 119–21.
5 Various dates are given for the onset of globalization:

Author	Start	Theme
Marx	15th century	modern capitalism
Wallerstein	15th century	capitalist world-system
Robertson	1870–1920	multidimensional
Giddens	18th century	modernization
Perlmutter	end of East–West conflict	global civilization

Cf. J. N. Pieterse, 'Globalization as Hybridization', in M. Featherstone, S. Lash and R. Robertson, eds, *Global Modernities*, London 1995, p. 47.
6 See A. Giddens, *Beyond Left and Right*, Cambridge 1994.
7 E. Altvater and B. Mahnkopf, 'Die globale Ökonomie am Ende des 20. Jahrhunderts', *Widerspruch*, 31, 1996, pp. 21ff.
8 A. D. Smith, *Nationalism in the Twentieth Century*, Oxford 1979, p. 191.

Chapter 1   The World Horizon Opens Up

1 Karl Marx and Friedrich Engels, 'Manifesto of the Communist Party', in Karl Marx, *The Revolutions of 1848* (Penguin/NLR edition), Harmondsworth 1973, p. 71.
2 In the Italian early Renaissance, for example, the concept of politics was closely bound up with that of society. See M. Viroli, *From Politics to Reasons*

of State: The Acquisition and Transformation of the Language of Politics, 1250–1600, Cambridge 1992, pp. 2ff.

3 See A. D. Smith, *Nationalism in the Twentieth Century*, Oxford 1979, pp. 191ff.

4 P. Alleyne-Dettmers, 'Tribal Arts: A Case Study of Global Compression in the Notting Hill Carnival', in J. Eade, ed., *Living the Global City*, London 1997, pp. 163–80.

5 L. Pries, 'Transnationale soziale Räume', *Zeitschrift für Soziologie*, 25/6, 1996, pp. 456–72; reprinted in U. Beck, ed., *Perspektiven der Weltgesellschaft*, Frankfurt/Main 1997.

6 Ibid., pp. 461ff.

7 For the following section, see also A. McGrew, 'A Global Society?', in S. Hall et al., eds, *Modernity and its Futures*, Cambridge 1992, pp. 61–116.

8 Immanuel Wallerstein, 'Klassenanalyse und Weltsystemanalyse', in R. Kreckel, ed., *Soziale Ungleichheiten, Soziale Welt*, special issue 2, Göttingen 1983, p. 303. Cf. I. Wallerstein, 'Culture as the Ideological Battleground of the Modern World-System', in M. Featherstone, ed., *Global Culture*, London 1990, pp. 35ff; and Wallerstein, *The Capitalist World-Economy*, Cambridge 1979.

9 Volker Bornschier has further developed and empirically grounded the world-system theory. See, most recently, V. Bornschier and B. Trezzini, 'Jenseits von Dependenz versus Modernisierungstheorie: Differenzierungsprozesse in der Weltgesellschaft und ihre Erklärung', in H.-P. Müller, ed., *Weltsystem und kulturelles Erbe*, Berlin 1996, pp. 53–79.

10 T. Wirth, 'Politik der Zukunft', in *Die Macht der Mutigen, Spiegel*, special issue 11, 1995, p. 8.

11 J. Rosenau, *Turbulence in World Politics*, Brighton 1990, p. 17.

12 On the following points, see McGrew, 'A Global Society?'

13 R. Gilpin, *The Political Economy of International Relations*, Princeton 1987, pp. 88, 85.

14 D. Held, *Democracy and the Global Order*, Cambridge 1995, p. 135.

15 See U. Beck, *Risk Society*, London 1992, and *World Risk Society*, Cambridge 1999.

16 See M. Zürn, 'Globale Gefährdungen und internationale Kooperation', *Der Bürger im Staat*, 45, 1995, p. 51, from which the ideas and data behind these typologies are taken.

17 The fact that such opportunities are also politically utilized, at least in part, is shown by the recent sharp rise in the number of international agreements and laws in this area. On the opportunities for 'globalization from below', see pp. 68–72; and on politicization through risks, pp. 98–101.

18 K. Robins, 'Tradition and Translation: National Culture and its Global Context', in J. Corner and S. Harvey, eds, *Enterprise and Heritage: Crosscurrents of National Culture*, London 1991, pp. 28ff.

19 Quoted from ibid., p. 29.

20 *Le Monde diplomatique*, April 1997.

21 See R. Robertson, *Globalization: Social Theory and Global Culture*, London 1992.

22 E. Beck-Gernsheim, 'Schwarze Juden und griechische Deutsche', in Beck, *Perspektiven der Weltgesellschaft*.

23 R. Robertson, 'Globalization', in M. Featherstone, S. Lash and R. Robertson, eds, *Global Modernities*, London 1995.

24 Ibid., p. 145.
25 On the following, see also McGrew, 'A Global Society?'
26 See below, Conclusion.
27 H. V. Perlmutter, 'On the Rocky Road to the First Global Civilization', in A. King, ed., *Culture, Globalization and the World System*, London 1991.
28 Is this differentiation between exclusive and inclusive distinctions typically *Western* or Eurocentric? Or can universal validity be claimed for it? Much suggests that the idea of a Both-And world society is a product of Western thought, which serves to mark out the position of Western metropolises or the Western point of reference for a world that has become global. Under the regime of a state-religious-cultural Either-Or, this conceptual world may – as J. Friedman writes – appear invasive and be treated accordingly. If a cultural space is unified in accordance with the Either–Or schema – whether by a hegemonic power or in the form of a hegemonic way of thinking and investigating – then spaghetti is (again) equated with Italian and a multiplicity of dialects become a 'national mother-tongue'. This means that cultural diversity is then rolled into gradual distinctions between correct and incorrect, normal and deviant. Cf. J. Friedman, 'Cultural Logics of the Global System', *Theory, Culture and Society*, 5, special issue on postmodernism, 1988, p. 458.
29 See A. Appadurai, 'Disjuncture and Difference in the Global Cultural Economy', in Featherstone, *Global Culture*, pp. 296–300.
30 K. Ohmae, *The Borderless World*, London 1990, pp. 18–19; A. D. Smith, 'Towards a Global Culture?', *Theory, Culture and Society*, 7, 1990, p. 177 – both quoted from S. Lash and J. Urry, *Economies of Signs and Space*, London 1994, pp. 307–8.
31 See Appadurai, 'Disjuncture and Difference'.
32 Z. Bauman, *Globalization*, Cambridge 1998, pp. 70, 72, 88, 96.
33 See below (pp. 64ff) the discussion of transnational civil society and the possibilities and necessities of cross-cultural criticism; also U. Beck, 'The Cosmopolitan Perspective', *British Journal of Sociology*, 1, 2000.
34 Already in the sixties Hannah Arendt raised this question in her book *Vita Activa*. See also U. Beck, *Brave New World of Work*, Cambridge 2000.
35 See also E. B. Kapstein, 'Workers and the World Economy', *Foreign Affairs*, May–June 1996, pp. 16–37.
36 Kommission für Zukunftsfragen, *Entwicklung von Erwerbstätigkeit und Arbeitslosigkeit in Deutschland und anderen frühindustrialisierten Ländern*, part 1, Bonn, October 1996.
37 A. B. Krüger, 'It's Time for Americans to Worry about Stagnation of Wages', *International Herald Tribune*, 1 August 1997, p. 8.
38 See below, ch. 5, 'Responses to Globalization'.

Chapter 2   Transnational Civil Society

1 See Elisabeth Beck-Gernsheim, 'Schwarze Juden und griechische Deutsche', in U. Beck, ed., *Perspektiven der Weltgesellschaft*, Frankfurt/Main 1997.
2 See U. Beck, *The Reinvention of Politics*, Cambridge 1997.

3 J. N. Pieterse, 'Globalization as Hybridization', in M. Featherstone, S. Lash and R. Robertson, eds, *Global Modernities*, London 1995, pp. 60–1.
4 Ibid., p. 50. The R. W. Cox quotation comes from 'Global Perestroika', in R. Miliband and J. Panitods, eds, *New World Order? Socialist Register*, London 1992, pp. 34ff.
5 S. Toulmin, *Cosmopolis: The Hidden Agenda of Modernity*, New York 1990, pp. 197–8.
6 See L. Pries, ed., *Internationale Migration*, special issue of *Soziale Welt*, Baden-Baden 1997.
7 Cf. M. Albrow, *The Global Age*, Cambridge 1996.
8 M. Hajer, 'Die Gestaltung der Urbanität', unpublished ms, Munich 1995.
9 See in this connection Jörg Dürrschmidt, *Individual Relevances in the Global-ized World*, dissertation, Bielefeld University, 1995; and John Eade, ed., *Living the Global City*, London 1997.
10 E. Beck-Gernsheim, *Was kommt nach der Familie?*, Munich 1998.
11 F. Nietzsche, *Werke in drei Bänden*, Munich 1994, vol. 1, p. 915.
12 Ibid., p. 874.
13 F. Nietzsche, *The Gay Science [Fröhliche Wissenschaft]*, no. 335, translated by Walter Kaufmann, New York 1974, p. 266.
14 G. E. Lessing, *Nathan the Wise*, III. vii, translated by W. A. Steel, London 1930, pp. 163, 168.
15 'History provides solid evidence that misunderstanding between different cultures is much more creative than understanding. Kirk Varnedoe [. . .], in his book *A Fine Disregard*, has demonstrated this by the wonderfully complicated ping-pong of misunderstandings which led to the influence of Japanese woodcuts upon Van Gogh and Degas. The Japanese in the sixteenth century built their elaborate art of wood-engraving upon a wrong understanding of the European principle of perspective. But that art in turn inspired Van Gogh and Degas to unleash the European artistic revolution of the twentieth century, which for its part began with a non-chalant modernist treatment of central perspective. It would appear, then, that understanding is precisely not the starting point and goal of a learning community functioning across different cultures.' S. Wackwitz, 'Alles hat seine Grenzen – Vom fragwürdigen Nutzen kultureller Lerngemeinschaf-ten', *Süddeutsche Zeitung*, 26 November 1996.
16 C. Bretherton, 'Universal Human Rights: Bringing People into Global Politics?', in C. Bretherton and G. Ponton, eds, *Global Politics*, Oxford 1996, p. 253.

Chapter 3   Contours of World Society

1 A. Nassehi, 'Die "Welt"-Fremdheit der Globalisierungsdebatte', *Soziale Welt*, 2, 1998, p. 154.
2 A. D. Smith, 'Towards a Global Culture?', in M. Featherstone, ed., *Global Culture*, London 1990, p. 180.
3 J. N. Pieterse, 'Globalization as Hybridization', in M. Featherstone, S. Lash and R. Robertson, eds, *Global Modernities*, London 1995, pp. 52–3.

4 Ibid., p. 53. (W. Rowe and V. Schelling quotation is from their *Memory and Modernity: Popular Culture in Latin America*, London 1991, p. 161.)
5 M. Shaw, *Civil Society and the Media in Global Crises*, London 1996, pp. 3–4.
6 See U. Beck, in idem, ed., *Kinder der Freiheit*, Frankfurt/Main 1997, pp. 347–61.
7 C. Bretherton, 'Universal Human Rights', in C. Bretherton and G. Ponton, eds, *Global Politics*, Oxford 1996, pp. 263–4.
8 See David Held, *Democracy and the Global Order*, Cambridge 1995, pp. 271–83.
9 Z. Bauman, *Globalization*, Cambridge 1998, p. 68.
10 See Laura Buffoni, 'Rethinking Poverty in Globalized Conditions', in J. Eade, ed., *Living the Global City*, London 1997, pp. 110–26.
11 For the following, see also U. Beck, *World Risk Society*, Cambridge 1999.
12 This is why there are still no insurance regulations for the new biological and genetic technologies. No one wants to cover the risks of biotechnology. So although no one may drive a car without third party insurance, the same is not required to run a genetic engineering installation.
13 See U. Beck, A. Giddens and S. Lash, *Reflexive Modernization: Politics, Tradition and Aesthetics in the Modern Social Order*, Cambridge 1994.
14 F. Nietzsche, *Werke in drei Bänden*, Munich 1994, vol. 2, p. 672.
15 M. Albrow, 'Auf dem Weg in eine globale Gesellschaft?', in U. Beck, ed., *Perspektiven der Weltgesellschaft*, Frankfurt/Main 1997.
16 P. G. Cerny, 'Globalization and the Changing Logic of Collective Action', *International Organization*, 49, 1995, p. 597.
17 J. Habermas, 'Jenseits des Nationalstaats?', in U. Beck, ed., *Politik der Globalisierung*, Frankfurt/Main 1997.
18 See above (pp. 66ff.) the distinction between culture (1) and culture (2).
19 See Eade, *Living the Global City*.
20 A. Bühl, *CyberSociety – Mythos und Realität der Informationsgesellschaft*, Cologne 1996. For a critical view, see Z. Sardar and J. R. Ravetz, eds, *Cyberfutures, Culture and Politics on the Information Superhighway*, London 1996.
21 The criticism of the container image of fenced-off individual societies is certainly aimed at the systems theory of Talcott Parsons. N. Luhmann introduced the concept 'world society' at an early date (see his 'Weltgesellschaft', in id., *Soziologische Aufklärung 2*, Opladen 1975, pp. 51–71). In his view, the emergence of world society has its roots in the logic of functional differentiation, which stops at no frontiers. What this means empirically, however, is an open question – as is whether it applies to transnational world societies. See also R. Stichweh, 'Zur Theorie der Weltgesellschaft', *Soziale Systeme*, 1995, pp. 29–45.
22 Albrow, 'Auf dem Weg in eine globale Gesellschaft?'
23 See above, pp. 3f.
24 Jean-Marie Guéhenno, *La fin de la démocratie*, Paris 1995, pp. 37, 38.
25 M. Mann, 'Hat Globalisierung den Siegeszug des Nationalstaats beendet?', *Prokla*, 106, 1997, pp. 113–41.
26 Habermas, 'Jenseits des Nationalstaats?'
27 This prospect and process of 'reflexive cosmopolitization is analysed in U. Beck, 'The Cosmopolitan Perspective. On the Sociology of the Second Age of Modernity', *British Journal of Sociology*, 1, 2000.
28 For further considerations on the transnational state, see below pp. 132ff.

Chapter 4   Errors of Globalism

1 U. Beck, 'The Cosmopolitan Perspective. On the Sociology of the Second Age of Modernity', *British Journal of Sociology*, 1, 2000.
2 See S. Lash and J. Urry, *The End of Organised Capitalism*, Cambridge 1987.
3 Far too little attention has been paid to the sharp *internal critique of management* expressed in *L'Horreur économique* (V. Forrester, Paris 1996) and *Witch Doctors* (J. Micklethwait and A. Wooldridge, New York 1996), or to the similar analyses of 'a school of thought in which there is an absence of thought' (J. Sur, *Une alternative au management: La mise en expression*, Paris 1996) and for which everything turns into money (R. Kuttner, *Everything for Sale*, New York 1997). For an overview, see O. Nigsch, 'Von der Soziologie zum Management. Und wieder zurück?', *Soziale Welt*, 4, 1997.
4 Kommission für Zukunftsfragen, *Bericht II: Erwerbstätigkeit in Deutschland: Entwicklung, Ursachen und Maßnahmen*, Bonn 1997, p. 111.
5 Ibid., pp. 111ff.
6 See P. Hirst and G. Thompson, 'The Problem of "Globalization": International Economic Relations, National Economic Management and the Formation of Trading Blocs', *Economy and Society*, 21/4, 1992.
7 M. Weber, 'Argentinische Kolonistenwirtschaften', in id., *Landarbeiterfrage, Nationalstaat und Volkswirtschaftspolitik. Schriften und Reden 1892–1899* (*Max Weber Gesamtausgabe*, part I, vol. 4.1), Tübingen 1993, p. 303.
8 For an overview, see ch. 1 of A. Giddens, *Beyond Left and Right*, Cambridge 1994.
9 See ch. 5, 'Responses to Globalization'.
10 Benjamin R. Barber, *Jihad vs McWorld: How Globalism and Tribalism are Reshaping the World*, New York 1996, p. 4.
11 See above pp. 42–7.
12 See below the section on an 'alliance for civil labour'.
13 *Schwarz*, the symbol of conservatism and of the Christian Democrat party in Germany, has been translated here either as 'black' (when the colour contrast with 'red' and 'green' is at the heart of the argument), or as 'conservative' or 'Christian Democrat' [*trans. note*].
14 Michael Zürn, 'Schwarz-Rot-Grün-Braun: Reaktionsweisen auf Denationalisierung', in U. Beck, *Politik der Globalisierung*, Frankfurt/Main 1997.
15 Ibid.
16 For details, see the report of the Kommission für Zukunftsfragen, Bericht I, Bonn 1996, pp. 5ff; and also U. Beck, *Brave New World of Work*, Cambridge 2000.
17 See e.g. Stephen A. Marglin and Juliet B. Schor, *The Golden Age of Capitalism*, Oxford 1990; or Elmar Altvater and Birgit Mahnkopf, *Grenzen der Globalisierung*, Münster 1997. For a detailed critique of this position, see also M. Zürn (n. 13 above).

Chapter 5   Responses to Globalization

1 O. Lafontaine, 'Globalisierung und internationale Zusammenarbeit', in U. Beck, *Politik der Globalisierung*, Frankfurt/Main 1997.

2 A. Giddens and C. Pierson, *Conversations with Anthony Giddens*, Cambridge 1998, pp. 172–3; A. Giddens, *The Third Way*, Cambridge 1998.

3 See U. Beck, *Brave New World of Work*, Cambridge 2000, last two chapters.

4 M. Jänicke, 'Umweltpolitik: Global am Ende oder am Ende global?', in Beck, *Politik der Globalisierung*.

5 See M. Mandelsbaum, *The Dawn of Peace in Europe*, New York 1996; and Robert J. Weber, ed., *Eagle Drift*, New York 1997.

6 See D. Archibugi, 'From the United Nations to Cosmopolitan Democracy', in D. Held, ed., *Cosmopolitan Democracy: An Agenda for a New World Order*, London 1995, pp. 121–35.

7 The further principle of a *common currency area* will not be analysed here because it has already been considered in the public debate over the euro. A common complaint is that only an economic Europe is envisaged in the drive towards the euro, but there is something to be said in favour of the view that a political Europe is willy-nilly developing as a result. Suddenly claims and interests affecting the labour market – the recognition of professional qualifications and craft diplomas, minimum wage levels, etc. – have to be harmonized within the common currency area. And hitherto national solidarities will expand into transnational solidarities – and conflicts!

8 This is also the basic idea in Kant's *Perpetual Peace*. See U. Beck, ed., *Kinder der Freiheit*, Frankfurt/Main 1997, pp. 147ff.

9 Herta Däubler-Gmelin, 'Globalisierung geht keineswegs Hand in Hand mit globalem Recht', *Frankfurter Rundschau*, 18 April 1997.

10 Archibugi, 'From the UN to Cosmopolitan Democracy', p. 156.

11 See below, 'Europe as a Response to Globalization'.

12 See F. W. Scharpf, 'Demokratie in der transnationalen Politik', in Beck, *Politik der Globalisierung*.

13 The new British Labour government under Tony Blair is beginning to take this principle to heart.

14 Robert B. Reich, *The Work of Nations*, London 1993, pp. 162, 163.

15 See H. Bollinger and W. Nothdurf, 'Schlüsselqualifikationen', manuscript, Fulda 1997.

16 R. Kahl, 'Globalisierung zwingt zu einer Reorientierung des Lernens', *tageszeitung*, 4 August 1997.

17 M. Brater, 'Schule und Ausbildung im Zeichen der Individualisierung', in Beck, *Kinder der Freiheit*, p. 153.

18 On the difficulties involved in various fiscal reforms, see Streeck, *Industrielle Beziehungen*. See also below, p. 159.

19 See above, pp. 45ff.

20 On social and environmental standards in world trade, see Frank Braßel and Michael Windfuhr, *Welthandel und Menschenrechte*, Bonn 1995; and Wolfgang Kreissl-Dörfler, ed., *Mit gleichem Maß – Sozial und Umweltstandards*, submissions by the Greens to the European Parliament, 1995.

21 See also Beck, *Brave New World of Work*.

22 For a more detailed discussion, see the section on 'civil labour' in Beck, *Brave New World of Work*.

23 I owe this reference to the Hans Knauth engineer's office in Meersburg.

24 Problems which they may perhaps not actually have.

25 See also above, pp. 139–40.

26 I owe this term to Barbara Adam.
27 H. Prantl, 'Probleme kann man nicht abschieben', *Süddeutsche Zeitung*, 20 May 1997, p. 27.
28 See U. Beck and E. Beck-Gernsheim, eds, *Riskante Freiheiten*, Frankfurt/ Main 1993; and Beck, *Kinder der Freiheit*.
29 See H. Wilkinson, 'Kinder der Freiheit', in Beck, *Kinder der Freiheit*, pp. 85– 123, and the new Shell Study, *Youth '97*.
30 J. Goebel and C. Clermont, 'Die Tugend der Orientierungslosigkeit', manuscript, Berlin 1997, pp. 22ff.
31 A. Zielcke, 'Der neue Doppelgänger', *Frankfurter Allgemeine Zeitung*, 20 July 1996.
32 See the report of the Kommission für Zukunftsfragen, 1996/1997; and Thomas Eckardt, *Arm in Deutschland*, Munich 1996.
33 All figures are taken from the OECD report of summer 1996 (as cited in the *Independent*, 4 April 1996).
34 Y. W. Bradshaw and M. Wallace, *Global Inequalities*, London 1996, pp. 16ff.
35 See the contributions in S. Leibfried and P. Pierson, eds, *Standort Europa. Europäische Sozialpolitik*, Frankfurt/Main 1997.
36 V. Post, 'Abschied vom Jammertal', *Die Zeit*, 28 March 1997.

Chapter 6   Europe and Globalization

1 Rolf Peter Sieferle, *Epochenwechsel – Die Deutschen an der Schwelle zum 21. Jahrhundert*, Berlin 1994, p. 78.
2 M. Kundera, *The Art of the Novel*, London 1988, p. 158.
3 J. Fischer, contribution to the discussion 'Heraus aus dem nationalen Biotop' [Out of the National Biotope], *tageszeitung*, 13 June 1997.
4 M. Greffrath, 'Die Frage nach dem New Deal', manuscript, Berlin 1997.

Index